# Blue Crabs

Catch 'em, Cook 'em, Eat 'em

by
Peter Meyer

Avian-Cetacean
Press

Published by Avian-Cetacean Press in Wilmington, NC.
Printed and bound in the United States of America.

All diagrams, illustrations, and photographs, unless otherwise credited, are by the author.

As with any endeavor of this type, mistakes or differences of opinion are bound to occur. Readers finding fault or disagreeing with the facts or opinions stated in *Blue Crabs: Catch 'em, Cook 'em, Eat 'em* are encouraged to share their facts or opinions with the author. Please direct comments to:

Peter Meyer
c/o Avian-Cetacean Press
PO Box 15643
Wilmington, NC 28408

Printing:    2   3   4   5   6   7   8   9   10

Library of Congress Card Number: 00-110310

**Publisher's Cataloging-in-Publication Data**
Meyer, Peter, 1952—
    Blue Crabs: Catch 'em, Cook 'em, Eat 'em/ by Peter Meyer
p. 128
Includes index and bibliography
ISBN: 0-9628186-3-1
1. Blue Crab  2. Crabbing  3. Cookery (Crabs)  4. Crabbing—Atlantic
    and Gulf Coasts (US)  I. Title
QL444.M33.M49 2003
595.38

                                                    00-110310
                                                    CIP

# Dedication

*Blue Crabs: Catch 'em, Cook 'em, Eat 'em* is dedicated to Cathy, Ben, and Jason Meyer, who have put up with the 'ol crab, Peter Meyer, for many years. With enthusiasm and good humor, Cathy, Ben, and Jason participated in various endeavors involving the capture, appreciation, preparation, and consumption of untold numbers of the species *Callinectes sapidus* (blue crabs).

In addition, my wife Cathy has been an integral part of the production of all "my" books. She deserves much credit for her professional assistance, from sharp-penciled editing to computerized bookkeeping.

# Disclaimer

The author presents opinions on the safe handling and eating of blue crabs and other marine species in *Blue Crabs: Catch 'em, Cook 'em, Eat 'em*. Every attempt has been made to present current safety standards for seafood consumption. Readers should nevertheless form independent opinions and maintain current knowledge on the safety of seafood handling, preparation and consumption.

# Introduction

*Blue Crabs: Catch 'em, Cook 'em, Eat 'em,* is a practical and entertaining guide for persons interested in blue crabs. The book is intended to be used and understood by the lay public. Significant effort, nevertheless, has been made to provide scientifically accurate information within the text.

The blue crab is a fascinating animal, deserving our respect and admiration. Yet, we humans prey on crabs. To revere yet consume blue crabs — does this represent a paradox? The answer is nay!

Crab fanciers seek and eat the blue crab, yet most do so with a deep regard and appreciation for *Callinectes sapidus.* To many, crabbing represents an enjoyable, almost magical endeavor.

Further, most crabbers fervently desire that humans actively conserve marine resources in order that future generations will continue to enjoy blue crabs.

# Contents

A Crabby Tale ................................................ 8
Why Crab? ................................................ 10

## Catch 'em! ..................................... 13
1- Crab pots ................................................ 13
2- Crab traps (hand traps) ........................ 16
3- Handlining ........................................ 19
4- Scapping ........................................ 21
5- Seining ........................................ 23
6- Trotlining ........................................ 25
Bait for Crabbing ........................................ 26
Where to Crab ........................................ 28
Salinity ........................................ 29
Time of Day ........................................ 29
Season to Crab ........................................ 29
Handling Crabs ........................................ 30
Crabbing Regulations ........................................ 31
Storing Crabs ........................................ 33
Crabpot Bycatch/Ghost Pots ........................................ 34

## Cook 'em! ..................................... 37
Picking Crabs ........................................ 39
Sharing the Crabbing Chores ........................ 42
Alternate Ways to Procure Crab Meat ............... 42
Using Crab Meat ........................................ 43
Freezing Crab Meat ........................................ 44

# *Eat 'em!* ............................ 45

Fresh Seafood is: ........................... 45
Nutrition — Blue Crab Meat ..................... 46

## Recipes

CREAM CHEESE CRAB DIP ..................... 47
CREAMY CRAB DIP ........................... 47
HOT CRAB DIP ............................. 48
CRAB SALAD DABS ........................... 49
CRAB SALAD ............................... 49
CRAB FINGERS ............................. 50
CRAB FEAST ............................... 51
CRAB PINEAPPLE DELIGHT ................... 52
CRAB SOUP ................................ 53
CRAB SANDWICHES .......................... 53
CRAB-CLAM RED CHOWDER .................... 54
CRAB-CLAM NEW ENGLAND CHOWDER ........... 55
CRAB AND CORN CHOWDER ................... 56
CRAB OMELET .............................. 57
CRAB CAKES I ............................. 58
CRAB CAKES II ............................ 59
CRAB CAKES III ........................... 59
CRAB SPAGHETTI ........................... 60
CRAB TOSTADAS ............................ 61
DEVILED CRAB ............................. 62
SEAFOOD GUMBO ............................ 63
CRAB AND SHRIMP JAMBALAYA ............... 64
CRAB NEW ORLEANS ........................ 65
CRAB CASSEROLE ........................... 66
CRAB-CHEESE CASSEROLE .................... 67
STUFFED FLOUNDER ......................... 68

# All About Blue Crabs ............69

Crustaceans/Crabs ...........................69
True Crabs .....................................72
Blue Crabs .....................................74
External Anatomy/Appearance .......................76
Internal Anatomy ...........................80
Life Cycle .....................................81
Molting.........................................84
Reproduction..................................86
Defense Mechanisms.......................88
Prey and Predators .........................90
Blue Crab Hitchhikers, Parasites, and Bacteria ..91

# Soft-Shell Crabs ......................... 93

Harvesting Soft-Shell Crabs..............94
Cleaning Soft-Shell Crabs ...............96
SOFT-SHELL CRAB SANDWICH RECIPE .........................97
GRILLED SOFT-SHELL CRABS ...........................98

# Commercial Crab Harvest .............. 99

Commercial Crabbing Methods ..................... 103

# Blue Crab Extras ........................... 107

Curious Crab Notes & Questions .......................... 108
Recommended Reading................................... 110
Recommended Websites................................ 111
State Crabbing Agencies ............................... 112
Tricky Crabby Terminology............................. 116
Definitions & Crab Terms ................................ 117
Scientific Names of Crab Species ............................ 121
Index........................................................ 122
From whence the title came ............................... 124
About the Author............................................. 125

# A Crabby Tale

Six year-old Jason pulled in the white string hand-over-hand. "Easy, guy, bring him up slowly," I advised.

"There he is, Jay!" Ben, age eight, pointed down into the water. "It's a big one!"

From the pea-green depths of the water rose a crab, clinging greedily to the fish head on the end of the string.

"Ready, Ben?" I said.

"Ready, Dad," Ben whispered.

Ben eased the six-foot-long dip net under the crab, then pulled upward with all his might. The net erupted from the surface, spewing water skyward like the eruption of a miniature, undersea volcano.

The green-shelled animal tangled within the net's mesh flailed its legs and claws, trying to escape. The crab's efforts were in vain. Ben eased his prize over the dock. He held the net high enough to inspect the underside of the crab.

"It's a male," he announced. "Keeper, Dad?"

"You bet," I replied. "He's a nice one."

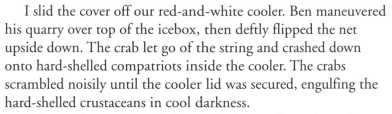

I slid the cover off our red-and-white cooler. Ben maneuvered his quarry over top of the icebox, then deftly flipped the net upside down. The crab let go of the string and crashed down onto hard-shelled compatriots inside the cooler. The crabs scrambled noisily until the cooler lid was secured, engulfing the hard-shelled crustaceans in cool darkness.

"That makes six," I said. "Enough for a crab spaghetti dinner and a crab omelet for breakfast, too. Who's going to help me clean these critters?"

"I will!" both boys yelled in unison.

In short order, the crabs had been cleaned, cooked, and picked (with help from Mom on the picking part). Later that evening, we sat enjoying a meal of crab spaghetti, a delectable dish unsurpassed by any gourmet concoction prepared for royalty.

Ben poked his fork at the last strands of white pasta on his plate. "Can we catch some more crabs tomorrow?" he asked.

I smiled, then did my best to scrunch my face and narrow my eyes in a proper adult, I'll-think-about-it look.

"Maybe we'll give the crabs a rest," I said, sopping up remnants of red sauce from my plate with a piece of bread. "But, how about if we see what kind of fish we can catch off the dock?"

"Yeah, Dad, let's go fishing," Ben said.

"Alllriight," Jason chimed in.

I winked at my wife. "Sometimes a Dad just has to do his duty."

"How about if Mom comes along to help tomorrow?" Cathy asked.

"Alllriight!" Ben, Jason, and I answered.

# Why Crab?

"Teach us to delight in simple things," said author Rudyard Kipling.

"The best things in life are free," sang the Rock 'n Roll group, the Kingsmen.

*Crabbing embodies the simple life.*

Kipling and the Kingsmen would have loved crabbing, for crabbing is an uncomplicated adventure, costing mere pennies, but reaping priceless rewards and fun.

Yet crabbing, especially crabbing with children, is more than just inexpensive entertainment. Crabbing educates youngsters, too. When children (and adults) go crabbing, they learn respect for the wonders of nature. They also acquire the ability to provide food for the table, and they can even become proficient at cooking the family's food.

Crabbing is a great way to enjoy the coastal environment. The pace of crabbing is unrushed, allowing ample time to enjoy the splendors of the coast — blue sky and cotton-white clouds overhead, skin-warming sunshine, hair-tousling breezes, soaring gulls and diving terns, and the fresh, sulfury aroma of the marsh.

Crab catchers also learn to appreciate the animal they seek. At first glance, a blue crab is a feisty, pugnacious, hard-shelled critter with a face only a mother crab could love. On closer inspection, a blue crab is a handsome animal, an awe-inspiring work of nature that is best appreciated by viewing the animal in its own salty environment.

- *A simple pleasure*
  - *Inexpensive*
    - *Fun for families and children*
      - *Educational – teaches about crabs and our coastal environment*

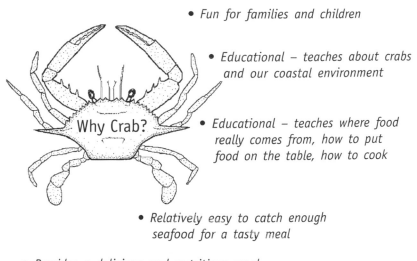

Why Crab?

- *Educational – teaches where food really comes from, how to put food on the table, how to cook*

- *Relatively easy to catch enough seafood for a tasty meal*

- *Provides a delicious and nutritious meal*

---

Through crabbing, overall environmental consciousness is also heightened — understanding is gained as to why humans need to protect the blue crab's environment. For indeed, is it not our own environment? Will we, too, not suffer if the hardy blue crab suffers? What person can spend a day crabbing and not want to protect our marine ecosystems?

On a more elemental level, crabbing is an easy way to catch enough food for a tasty crab concoction. The sweet taste of crab meat is well worth the effort involved in catching, cleaning, and picking a batch of these hard-bodied crustaceans. And, as with other foods, crab meals just seem to taste better if the chefs catch their own crabs.

Catching, cleaning, and preparing our food also puts us back in touch with our place on the planet. In purchasing a piece of chicken or fish at the grocery store, we adults and children lose sight of where food comes from. In preparing our own crabs, it becomes apparent that food doesn't just magically appear in the grocery store aisles.

For children and adults, catching and cooking a kettle of crabs engenders fun and joy, a feeling of accomplishment, an appreciation of nature's glory, a sense of place in the world, and satiated stomachs.

*Crabbing is "child's play," an excellent way for children to enjoy and learn about their environment.*

*A family crabbing outing, whether from a dock, boat, or the bank of a marsh creek, provides priceless vacation and/or childhood memories.*

# Catch 'em!
## How to Catch Blue Crabs

Several techniques can be used to nab crabs. The six most common methods include: 1) using crab pots, 2) using crab traps (hand traps), 3) handlining, 4) scapping, 5) seining, and 6) trotlining.

### 1– Crab pots

Catching crabs with a crab pot is generally easier and more successful than with other crabbing methods. Crab potting, in fact, might be called the lazy man's method of harvesting tasty crustaceans.

The crab pot was invented by B. F. Lewis of Harryhogan, Virginia, in the 1920's. Lewis patented an improved version of his crab pot in 1938. The new design revolutionized the crabbing industry. The same basic design is still widely used today.

A crab pot is a cage-like box (picture below) made from steel wire galvanized with zinc. The wire is often coated with plastic for added protection. The wire is formed into walls of one- to two-inch-wide hexagons. A typical pot measures 2 feet wide, 2 feet deep, and 18 inches high.

*A typical crab pot.*

A wire partition divides the box into an upper section and lower section (picture below). A wire bait basket, cylindrical in shape, is secured in the middle of the lower section. Funnel-like openings in each side of the lower section allow crabs to enter the pot easily, but exit the pot only with difficulty. Two more funnel-like openings allow crabs to move from the lower section into the upper section.

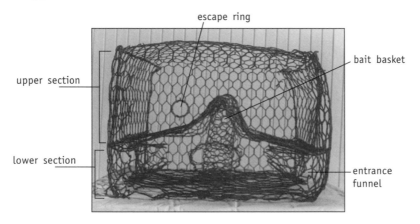

*Anatomy of a crab pot.*

A rope is securely tied to the top of the crab pot. Weight, such as bricks or a metal reinforcing bar (rebar), is often secured to the bottom of the crab pot. The added weight serves to keep the crab pot on the bottom of the sound when crabbing.

Bait (any type of whole fish, fish carcasses, chicken parts, or other meat) is placed in the bait basket.

A crab pot can be set (put in place) from a dock or boat. If the pot is placed off a dock, the near end of the rope is secured to a cleat or piling. If the pot is placed in open water, off a boat, a Styrofoam float is tied to the near end of the rope. The float bobs on the surface, marking the spot where a pot is located. A name and/or boat registration number on the buoy identifies the owner of the pot.

The crab pot sits submerged on the bottom, in a location that remains under water even at low tide (crabs will dehydrate and die if left exposed to the sun for too long). Ample rope must be allowed for the water to rise at high tide without pulling the pot off the bottom.

When crabs smell the bait in a crab pot, they crawl into the bottom section of the pot to feed on the bait. Since blue crabs have a tendency to move upward, they gravitate into the upper chamber, where they can no longer feed on the bait (so the bait lasts longer).

Small holes called escape or cull rings in the sides of the pot allow smaller crabs to escape from the upper chamber. Larger crabs are trapped until a crabber harvests the catch. The crabs are harvested by unhooking a latch on one side of the top of the pot, turning the pot upside down, and shaking the crabs out of the pot.

Letting a crab pot sit overnight garners more crabs because blue crabs tend to feed at dusk and dawn. The pot should be harvested at least once every 24 hours, or else the crabs begin to cannibalize each other. Checking the pot and adding new bait twice a day can increase the catch significantly, as well.

Half-high crab pots (picture below) have only one section — they are not divided into upper and lower sections. Because crabs consume bait the entire time they are trapped in half-high pots, bait is used up more quickly than with standard pots. Also, crabs can escape from half-high pots more easily. Thus, half-high pots should be tended more often than standard crab pots. Checking the pots every few hours works best.

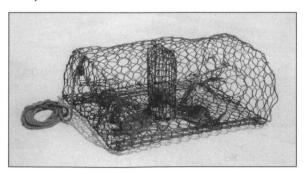

*Half-high crab pot.*

Using a crab pot might not be as much fun or challenging as other crabbing methods, but it is productive, time-wise. Professional crabbers, in fact, use crab pots — but, instead of one or two pots, professional crabbers use a large number of pots.

As an amateur crabber, if all one seeks is delectable white crab meat to use in favorite recipes, a crab pot works well. If fun is part of the crabbing goal, use another method, or use another method combined with a crab pot as a backup.

## 2– Crab traps (hand traps)

Small, collapsible pyramid, box, or hoop (basket) wire traps (pictures below) are also used to snare crabs.

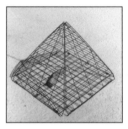
Pyramid trap.

Box trap.

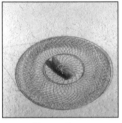
Hoop trap.

These traps share many common features.

Bait is securely tied to the bottom of the traps. The traps are tossed into the water and eased down onto the mud or sand bottom. When the traps come to rest on the bottom, the sides of the traps collapse downward/outward, leaving a flat, wire surface with bait in the middle.

Crabs crawl onto the traps to feed on the bait. Crabs can come and go as they please. However, when the rope is pulled, the walls of the traps come up. The traps resume their original pyramid/box/hoop (basket) shape, and the crab is trapped inside, unable to flee.

The bait should be tied *securely* to the bottom of the cages, so a crab cannot scurry off with the bait. These crab traps should be checked about every 15 minutes (the traps need to be tended on a nearly continuous basis).

## Pyramid/Box Traps

Pyramid and box traps (pictures below) work best on flat surfaces. They will still open if small rocks or debris lie on the bottom, but if large objects are present, the sides of the cage might not open, resulting in reduced crabbing success.

When checking these traps, the rope should be jerked hard at first, in order to close the sides of the cage quickly.

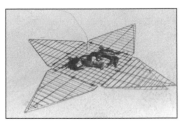

*Pyramid trap resting on the bottom, sides open.*

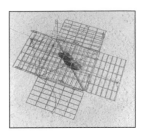

*Box trap resting on the bottom, sides open.*

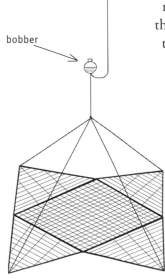

bobber

Placing a fishing bobber on the rope of a pyramid or box trap allows the trap to work more smoothly. A two-inch fishing bobber is attached to the main pull line of the trap, about one foot from where the line attaches to the trap (diagram left). The bobber prevents the lines attached to the sides of the cage from getting snagged on the bottom.

Pyramid-shaped traps fold down more readily than box-shaped traps, making transport and storage easier.

17

## Hoop (Basket) Traps

Open, hoop-type traps consist of a smaller-diameter ring inside a larger-diameter ring. The rings are connected by netting.

Hoop nets work in a manner similar to pyramid and box traps. When a hoop-type trap is placed on the bottom, the trap

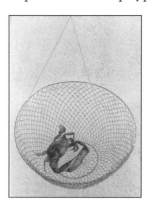

lies flat. Crabs crawl onto the trap and feed on the bait. When the string to the trap is pulled, the top ring rises first. The two rings and netting form a basket in which the crab is imprisoned. The basket is open on top; the pull of the trap to the surface should be continuous, strong, and steady, lest the crab escape out this opening.

Hoop traps are simple to use, inexpensive, and lie flat in storage. However, hoop traps work well only in calm waters with a flat bottom.

*Hoop (basket) trap.*

*Crab traps provide an advantage when crabbing from a high bridge or dock, where a dip net can't reach the water. Crabs drop off a baited hand line once they are pulled out of the water. Pyramid, box, and hoop traps insure that crabs won't escape.*

## 3– Handlining

Handlining is a more-work-but-more-fun method of crab-catching. A handline (picture below), also known as a dropline, consists of a small piece of wood, a string, and a weighted fastener or clip. A long-handled net, known as a dip net or scoop net, is used to snatch crabs off the dropline.

Heavy string, about 20 feet long, is utilized for a handline. A large, sturdy clip, one that can secure a fish head or chicken neck, is attached to one end of the string. A piece of wood is tied to the other end. The line is coiled around the wood for storage and transport.

*Handline for crabbing.*

To use the handline, bait is securely attached to the clip. The string is unwound, and the baited clip is thrown into any brackish water.

After throwing a baited line, the near end of the line is secured. The line can be tied to a cleat or piling on a dock, or to a boat fitting. If crabbing from shallow water, the line can be tied to a long stick or pole; the stick or pole is pushed into the sandy bottom to secure the stick in place.

To "fish" with a handline, hold the line between the thumb and index finger. Tug gently on the line every so often. If line tightening, gentle return tugs, or to-and-fro movements are felt, a crab is sampling the bait. The line feels "alive" because the crab's grabbing, pinching, and chewing on the bait is being transmitted up the string.

When such movement is felt, pull the string slowly and steadily. Don't make loud noises or sudden, jerking movements.

Continue to reel in the line slowly and easily, until the crab is close. Do not lift the bait out of the water while the crab is still holding on — the crab will likely drop the bait, plop back in the water, and swim away swiftly.

19

Use a long dip net to capture the crab. Choose one of two techniques: 1) Put the net down in the water before the crab comes into view. As the crab rises above the net, jerk the net sharply upward, capturing the crustacean. 2) Hold the net ready until the crab comes into view. When the crab is close enough, thrust the net under the crab and lift upward — all in one fell swoop.

*Handliner with dip net at ready.*

Dip nets typically have handles from three to six feet long. Short-handled nets are easier for children to manage. Long-handled nets, which reach more crabs, are more easily used by older children and adults. Extra-long dip nets, 12 feet or more in length, are utilized while crabbing on bridges.

The netting in dip nets is made from cotton, nylon, or wire. Wire nets are more expensive, but crabs are more easily extracted from wire mesh.

Good locations for handlining are under a dock, beside a bridge, or on the shores of a tidal creek. Handlines can also be tossed from a boat.

The handline technique provides more enjoyment if small children are thrown into the equation. Watching children learn to work together, and seeing them bask in their crabbing success, is ample reward in itself.

Using several handlines per child keeps the action lively and the interest level higher. Use as many lines as each child can easily watch. However, many lines too close together results in tangles and frustration.

When water current is strong, a lead sinker should be attached near the clip of a handline. The weight keeps the bait on the bottom, where the bait can best attract crabs. The more current, the heavier the weight required. A sinker should be used only when necessary. The weight makes it a little more difficult to feel a crab working a line and a little harder to pull the line up smoothly. Similarly, a too-large-and-heavy piece of bait will reduce the feel of crab impulses transmitted up a handline.

## 4— Scapping

Scapping is the minimalist method of snaring crabs. Scapping uses no bait and little equipment, so it is the least expensive crabbing technique. The only requirements are a keen eye, a swift hand, and a long-handled dip net.

Blue crabs are often visible clinging to pilings or other submerged structures adjacent to docks. They can also be spotted scooting along a muddy bottom in shallow water. Eelgrass beds often hide peelers and soft-shell crabs, in addition to hard crabs.

A swift scoop with a dip net can capture such crabs. The jab and scoop must be lightning quick, as blue crabs move surprisingly fast when threatened.

Cooperation between two scappers, each using a dip net, makes scapping more successful and more fun. When a crab is spotted, both scappers stand ready. One scapper dips straight for the crab. The other scapper covers the crab's back-door escape route with the second net.

Scapping can be done from a dock, while wading through shallow water on foot, or while boating slowly through shallow water.

*Successful scappers.*

Daytime scapping can be used to augment crabs obtained by handlining. Areas where fishermen clean fish are especially prone to attract scappable crabs.

Night scapping follows the same pattern as day scapping, except a strong light from a lantern or large flashlight is employed. A headlamp (picture right) works especially well, since hands remain free to handle scapping and other tasks. Lights of any type seem to attract and mesmerize crabs, facilitating their capture.

*Headlamp.*

Children especially enjoy nocturnal crabbing. Kids love an outside, nighttime adventure. As a bonus, all sorts of interesting critters inhabiting inky, nighttime waters are discovered and observed with a bright light.

Night crabbing boasts another advantage — beating the heat in hot, summertime weather. Bug spray is essential, however, if the wind is calm, as insects can be bothersome.

*Nighttime scapping.*

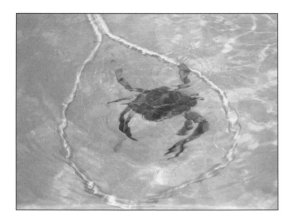

*On occasion, floaters, blue crabs floating with the current or swimming on top of the water, are spotted. Floaters can be scapped right off the surface of the water with a dip net.*

## 5– Seining

Seining is another baitless way to catch crabs. A hand-held seine net is utilized. The hand seine is a long, fine-mesh net, tied to wooden poles (diagram below). Styrofoam or cork floats are spaced along the top of the net; lead weights are spaced across the bottom of the net.

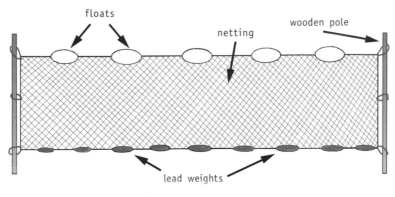

*Seine net components.*

Using a seine net means getting wet, at least from the waist down.

Two people are required to use a hand seine. Each person takes a pole. The poles are pushed in front of the seiners as they walk forward through shallow water. The floats hold the top edge of the net on the surface. The lead weights keep the lower edge of the net on the bottom. The swath of net between the floats and weights captures anything in its path.

*Using a seine net: The poles are pushed in front of the seiners.*

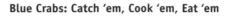 

At the end of a "pull," the net is pushed up onto shore and laid on the ground. The catch is then examined. Large, keeper crabs are placed in a cooler or bucket; smaller crabs are returned to the water.

A bonus of seining for hard-shell blue crabs is capturing various tiny fish, shrimp, snails, other species of crabs, soft-shell blue crabs, and even an occasional large fish in the net. Part of the fun of seining is seeing what exciting "prizes" turn up in each pull of the net.

Seining also demonstrates that marsh-adjacent waters are, indeed, the "nursery of the sea." Baby fish, tiny crabs, and small shrimp abound in the catch, for these animals literally grow up in sound waters. These miniature critters should be returned to the water promptly, or else they die.

A key to successful seining is keeping the poles on the bottom during a pull. If the net moves off the bottom, creatures escape underneath the net.

Old, sturdy shoes, ones that will not be pulled off feet in marsh mud, are essential. Shoes protect toes from pinching crabs; more importantly, shoes prevent cuts on the feet from oyster shells, rocks, and broken glass.

Regulations on seining should be checked in each state. States vary in rules on the length of net allowed, licensing, and the number of crabs, shrimp, etc., that can be taken by seine net.

*Seine net catch.*

## 6– Trotlining

Trotlining is a crab-catching method used infrequently today. Commercial crabbers used trotlines extensively in times past, before the introduction of more efficient crab pots.

A trotline (diagram below) consists of a long strand of rope, from a hundred feet to a mile in length. Hooks are not used. Instead, tough, inexpensive pieces of bait, such as pieces of eel or fish heads, are tied to the rope every three to four feet. Heavy chains anchor both ends of the rope and keep the trotline on the bottom. A floating buoy marks each end of the trotline.

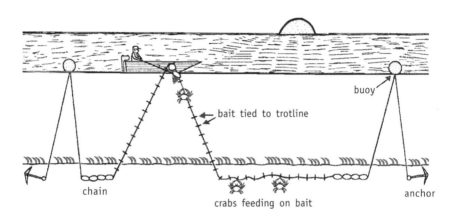

*Crab trotline.*

A trotline is set daily by boat. The line is laid on the bottom in sound waters. The line is "run" every hour or so to catch crabs.

To run the line, the crabber pulls one end of the baited line up to the boat. The boat then progresses down the line, the crabber working bait-to-bait until the end of the line is reached. Crabs clinging to the bait are caught with a dip net. A trotliner must work quickly: A crab must be scooped, deposited in a crab basket in the boat, and the net immediately readied for the next crab.

The trotline is worked by going with tidal flow, not against it.

## Bait for Crabbing

Crabs aren't especially picky when it comes to their diet. Clearly though, some foods are better than others to attract crabs. Meat (animal flesh) is, by far, the best crab bait.

Whole fish, fish heads, and chicken parts are common crab baits. Any type of meat, though, can be utilized: turkey wings, venison parts, shrimp heads, cow tongues, clams, leftover pieces of hot dog, hamburger, steak, etc. — all can go into the crab pot.

For handlining, the easier that a piece of meat ties onto a line, the better it works. Fish heads work well: The string can go right through the fish's mouth, assuring that the bait is held in place securely. The tougher a piece of meat is, the harder a crab will have to work to eat it — and the longer the bait will last.

Chicken remnants, such as backs, necks, and wing tips, make good bait for handlines or traps. Scrap poultry parts are obviously easier on the pocketbook than prime pieces. Less-expensive, whole chickens can be purchased for meals, with the back, neck, and other unwanted parts being used fresh — or frozen for future crabbing.

Menhaden or other oily fish (mackerel, bluefish, eel) are preferred over non-oily fish by many commercial crabbers for bait in crab pots. Almost any fish will work, however.

Large fish carcasses make excellent and long-lasting bait. Remains can be obtained at little or no cost from fish markets or from friends who have caught king mackerel or other offshore gamefish. The fish bodies are often too big to fit in the bait basket of a crab pot, but they can be thrown into the upper section of the pot. There, the carcasses will provide bait for three to four days of crabbing.

Typically, crabs prefer fresh bait over old, spoiled bait. Freezer-stored bait, though, works just as well as fresh bait.

Because of the tendency of recreational crabbers to use chicken necks for bait, commercial crabbers sometimes call amateur crabbers "chicken neckers." The term can be used in a derogatory fashion, as some commercial crabbers feel their livelihood is threatened by weekend, amateur crabbers.

Fish heads or whole fish
make excellent crab bait.

Chicken parts of any type
readily attract crabs.

Shrimp heads can be stuffed
into a mesh bag.

The bag of shrimp heads is
placed into the bait well.

photo by Ben Meyer

"Kissing the bait" is a tradition
begun by watermen, the
hardy people who make a
living from the sea.
Smooching the bait before
placing it in a crab trap is
said to generate a good
harvest of blue crabs.

## Where to Crab

Blue crabs inhabit waters all the way from the salty ocean to freshwater tidal rivers, miles upstream from the sea. Mostly, though, blue crabs are found in brackish water. Brackish water is a mixture of salt and fresh water, found in estuaries (areas where salt and fresh water meet) and sounds.

Shallower waters, between 10 and 15 feet maximum depth, and quiet waters, with less current, provide optimal crabbing. Deeper water and high-current areas harbor fewer crabs and also are more difficult locations in which to crab.

Bottom vegetation, docks, pilings, and bridge foundations all give crabs a place to hide, and make for good crabbing. Locations where fish are cleaned and the scraps thrown into the water, such as fish markets or fish cleaning stations, also harbor good-sized crabs.

Favorable crabbing locales can be found by asking for advice at bait shops. Other crabbers, too, can be queried. Good crabbing spots are generally not guarded like prime fishing spots. Sometimes, just watching to see where other people are crabbing, especially *successfully* crabbing, is the best way to find crabbing locations.

Optimal water depth for crabbing varies from place-to-place and time-of-year. Crabbing at different locations might be necessary: If shallow water sites result in a harvest of small crabs, deep water locations will likely yield larger crabs.

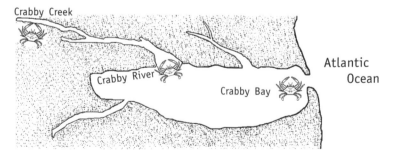

*Blue crabs can be caught anywhere from salty ocean inlets to freshwater tidal creeks.*

## Salinity

Salinity (the amount of salt) in crab-laden waters ranges from 36/1000 (36 parts salt per thousand parts water) in the ocean to 0/1000 in fresh water. The gender of crabs and the time of year both bear a relationship to the salinity in which crabs can be successfully harvested.

In springtime, both male and female crabs are found in sound and bay waters of lower salinity. In autumn, females move toward ocean inlets to release their eggs. Thus, in the fall months, females are more abundant in deeper water areas, nearer ocean inlets, while nice-sized jimmies (males) make up most of the catch in low-salinity waters.

## Time of Day

Early morning is a great time to crab if a crabber can rise and shine at dawn. Mid-day, with high sun and hot temperatures, is generally a slower crabbing time.

Crabs are active at night, so setting pots overnight often results in a good harvest.

## Season to Crab

Crab-catching can be accomplished most of the year. Only in cold winter months are crabs unavailable.

The peak abundance of crabs occurs in the warmer months, when water temperature has increased. Optimal water temperature for crabbing is from 62° to 80°F.

Perhaps the best time to harvest large, meaty crabs is in the late fall. Females have migrated toward deeper water and ocean inlets by autumn. Large, male crabs remain behind. A crab pot placed in brackish water often comes up loaded with good-sized jimmies.

The length of the annual crabbing season correlates with geographic location and climate: the farther north, the shorter the crabbing season. Conversely, the farther south, the longer the season.

In northern waters, crabs hibernate during the winter months. When water temperatures drop below 40°F, crabs bury themselves in a muddy or sandy bottom and enter into a dormant state.

Farther south, in Florida and Gulf Coast waters, blue crabs might not take a mud rest at all. Instead, they go through a period of decreased activity in the colder months.

## Handling Crabs

Crabs can pinch a person's fingers or toes with surprising force. The pinch often punctures or slices the skin and draws blood.

To avoid a harsh pinch, pick up a crab safely: Hold the crab at the rear of its shell. Grasp the crab between the last pair of legs (the swim-paddles). Be careful that fingers don't extend too far under the crab. The crab can reach under its body and deliver a powerful pinch.

Picking up a crab by gently grasping its swim-paddles (picture below, left) is another safe alternative. Held by its swim paddles, a crab cannot extend its claws far enough backward to pinch one's fingers. Heavy, canvas gloves (picture below, right) also provide protection from crab pinches.

*Picking a crab up safely by grasping the crab's swim paddles.*　　*Heavy, canvas gloves can also protect fingers from a crab's pinch.*

Long-handled, metal tongs (picture below, left) can be used to safely handle crabs. The clack-clack of an angry crab pinching the tongs provides ample incentive for keeping one's fingers clear of those powerful claws. Tongs make crab-handling much safer for young children, too.

If a blue crab is scurrying about, a sneaker-clad foot can be lightly pressed onto the top of the crab's shell (picture below, right) to recapture the escapee. Don't try this maneuver barefoot!

Metal tongs can be used to handle blue crabs safely.

A shoe, placed lightly on a crab's shell, can hold it in place.

## Crabbing Regulations

To protect and preserve fish and wildlife, all states have enacted laws and regulations. Each state with blue crabs in its waters has specific statutes governing the harvest of crabs by both commercial and amateur crabbers.

Amateur crabbers must learn the rules in any crabbing location *before* going crabbing. Amateur crabbing regulations vary from state-to-state. Some states require an inexpensive license for amateur crabbers. Most states limit the size of crabs and the number of crabs that can be taken. Many states set a limit on crabbing equipment, also.

Each state has a regulatory agency responsible for posting and enforcing crabbing regulations. Crabbers should contact the appropriate agency to learn the regulations in the state in which they will be crabbing (state agency addresses, phone numbers, and websites are listed on pages 112-115).

Generally, hard crabs measuring five inches or more can be legally harvested; smaller crabs are throwbacks. Size is measured tip-to-tip, from the lateral spine tip on one side of a crab to the lateral spine tip on the opposite side (technically, the width of the crab is measured, even though the measurement is sometimes called the length of the crab).

The five-inch keeper rule also makes sense from a picking standpoint: Bigger crabs have more meat.

Many measuring devices, from a ruler to calipers to gap devices (pictures below), can be used to measure blue crabs. With experience, a crabber develops a reliable "crabeye," and keepers can be separated from throwbacks at a glance.

Homemade crab measuring device with a five-inch gap.

Yardstick used to make sure a crab measures five inches from point-to-point.

Most states prohibit the harvest of sponge (egg-laden female) crabs: Crabbers should return all sponge crabs to the water immediately. Common sense (and scientific evidence from other species) dictates that returning egg-laden crabs to the water should help sustain an adequate crab population.

Upon returning a sponge crab to the water, tell her, "Go free, lass, so you can make more crabs to fill the brine."

Some states restrict harvesting *any* female crab, again in an attempt to conserve the resource.

Recently-shed (but hard) crabs can be returned to the wild, too. If a crab feels light, and a glance at its bottom shows a bright-white shell, the specimen has recently shed. A less-than-full complement of meat will be present inside its new shell.

## Storing Crabs

Freshly-caught crabs must be kept alive until they are cooked. A hard and fast rule of safe crab consumption is to cook only live crabs — cooking dead crabs, much like cooking dead clams and oysters, invites the seafood GI (gastrointestinal) blues.

Freshly-caught crabs can't just be thrown into the bottom of a boat or crowded into a water-filled, five-gallon bucket; they'll soon die.

A bushel basket can be used to keep crabs alive while crabbing, as long as the crabs are kept wet. Drape a piece of burlap or towel over the crabs. Wet the cloth frequently by pouring water on top of it, soaking the crabs at the same time. Placing the bushel basket in shade helps to keep the crabs alive, as well.

*A bushel basket used to store crabs.*

A five-gallon bucket with numerous holes drilled in it can also be used to keep crabs alive. Pour water on the crabs (or dunk the whole bucket in water) frequently to keep the crabs wet. As an alternative, the whole bucket can be tied to a dock cleat and left completely immersed in water.

Crabs should not be kept in standing water. If crabs are kept in a water-filled bucket, the water must be changed very frequently to replenish the oxygen in the water and to keep the water from getting too warm.

*A five-gallon bucket used to store crabs.*

Crabs can also be kept alive by cooling them. Crabs remain viable up to 48 hours if they are stored in a cooler or refrigerator. Cooling crabs has the added advantage of rendering them easier to handle: A strong-clawed, warrior crab becomes a slow-moving, docile crustacean when cooled.

When crabs are kept in a cooler, they should be kept *on top of* ice: If immersed in ice water, crabs die.

*Crabs stored in a cooler should be kept **on top of** the ice, not under the ice.*

When storing crabs, soft-shell crabs should never be mixed with their hard-shell cousins; the hard-skinned members will feast on their soft-skinned kin.

## Crabpot Bycatch/Ghost Pots

Catching blue crabs is the primary goal of setting a crab pot. Hard-shell and soft-shell crabs are the usual captives in crab pots, but other critters are sometimes snared, as well. Part of the fun of

setting a crab pot is checking to see what is the "catch of the day".

Pinfish, croakers, flounder, puffers, grouper, whelk, spider crabs, and stone crabs are a few of the more common "bycatch" species captured in a crab pot. Many of these fish and crabs are edible, assuming they are large enough to clean. Such incidental harvest is generally legal, but state regulations should be checked prior to utilizing bycatch from crab pots.

*Flounder bycatch from a crab pot.*

*Common bycatch in crab pots: pinfish, croaker, and stone crabs.*

Diamondback terrapins frequently enter crab pots in search of food. Sometimes, like crabs, the turtles are trapped inside. Because the turtles are air-breathing reptiles, they drown if they are unable to swim out of the pots. Countless terrapins die annually in this manner. Crab pots, in fact, are likely a significant factor keeping terrapin populations far below past levels of abundance.

Scientists are currently working on designing crab pots with TED's (Turtle Excluder Devices). One TED consists of a two by five inch rectangular, stainless steel wire, attached to the inner opening of each crab pot funnel. Studies have shown that while the device successfully excludes turtles, the crab catch

*Diamondback terrapins are sometimes trapped in crab pots.*

with such pots remains the same or actually increases. Hopefully, TED's on crab pots will become standard issue one day soon, enabling terrapin populations to expand. Until then, crabbers can help conservation efforts by checking crab pots several times a day. Hopefully, turtles can be released before they die.

Otters are also trapped in crab pots on occasion. Otters, being air-breathing mammals, also perish if they cannot escape.

*Diamondback terrapins often die if they become trapped in crab pots.*

Ghost pots present another blue crab conservation challenge. Ghost pots are crab pots which have been accidentally lost or just abandoned by recreational or commercial fishermen. These pots continue to trap crabs, terrapins, and even fish, many of which needlessly perish. Designs which allow the breakdown of a larger escape ring after a crab pot is in the water for a certain length of time are promising. For now, crabbers can help by removing ghost pots from sound waters. The pots can be put back to use or disposed of properly.

*Abandoned "ghost pots" in the marsh.*

*The inevitable result of ghost pots — dead crabs.*

# Cook 'em!
## How to Cook Blue Crabs

With any crab-catching method, little time and effort is usually required to gather enough crabs for a delicious feast. A mere four crabs can be used to make a tasty dish like crab spaghetti (recipe page 60). Even a single crab will provide enough meat for a delicious crab omelet (recipe page 57).

As with any seafood, the fresher the supply, the better the taste. Catching one's own crabs ensures a fresh supply and optimal taste.

Wash crabs before cooking them. Spray the crabs with a water hose while they are in a bucket. Pour off the water after spraying.

**Cook only live crabs. Dead crabs should be discarded in order to avoid food-associated illness.**

RIP - Do not eat!

*Dead crabs should never be eaten.*

Crabs are most often cooked by boiling or steaming. Fervent proponents of both methods exist.

To boil crabs, bring a large pot of water to a brisk boil. Allow enough water to completely cover the crabs. Using tongs, pick up the crabs and drop them in the pot one-by-one. Return the water to boiling, then cook the crabs at a gentle boil for ten minutes.

After cooking, drain the hot water. Cover the crabs with cold water for one minute. Pour off the water, then cover the crabs once more with cold water. Let the crabs sit in the cold water five to ten minutes. Drain the water once more. The crabs are now ready to pick.

**Never let cooked crabs come into contact with uncooked crabs. Never put cooked crabs in a container in which live crabs have been stored unless the container is thoroughly cleaned. Otherwise, *Vibrio* or other marine bacteria from the uncooked crabs could contaminate the cooked crabs and potentially cause illness in humans (any bacteria present on uncooked crabs are killed during the cooking process).**

To steam crabs, again use a large pot. Put an inch or two of water in the pot and bring the water to a boil. Place the crabs in the steamer basket. Steam the crabs for 20 minutes. Remove the crabs from the pot. Dump the crabs on a paper-covered table if a crab feast is taking place. Otherwise, allow the crabs to cool before picking.

One advantage of steaming is that the crabs are easier to clean. Boiled crabs are full of hot water when they're done. Steamed crabs emit fewer dribbles of water when they are cracked open.

*Options to add to crab boil water.*

Spices or beer in the water are optional with either the boiling or steaming method of cooking crabs. One advantage of adding spices is that the smell of cooking crabs is rendered more pleasant. Lemon juice and vinegar are other crab-boil options.

Contrary to what is stated in many crab-cooking instructions, crabs are *not* done when they turn red. Crabs actually turn red shortly after being deposited in boiling water.

Another technique of preparing and cooking crabs involves cleaning crabs prior to cooking them. Chilling the crabs first makes this method easier (crabs are docile at cooler temperatures) and more humane. Kill each crab, using a quick stab with an ice pick, aimed behind and between the crab's eyes. Remove the top shell, apron, gills and internal organs. Cook the already-cleaned crabs by boiling or steaming.

Proponents of this clean-before-cooking method suggest that 1) spices added to the water can seep deeper into the crab meat, providing better taste, and 2) the mess generated with this method is less than the mess associated with picking and eating whole, cooked crabs.

## Picking Crabs

Crabs should be cooked before they are picked. Removing raw meat from blue crabs is far more difficult than picking the meat from cooked crabs.

Actual picking methods vary. What works well for one person might not go smoothly for another. Picking crabs is part art form, part science.

Truly, no one will ever confuse picking blue crabs with picking up fast food (thank goodness!). Time, patience, and persistence are essential elements of picking crabs. The task is labor intensive.

Picking is an activity that goes easier in the company of family or friends. Visiting, talking, and picking each other's brains at the same time the crabs are being picked makes the chore much easier. As an alternative, put on some favorite music and enjoy "picking and grinning."

The goal in picking a crab is to remove the succulent, white, muscle meat from the crab's shell and claws. Perhaps the best way to acquire picking proficiency is by having an experienced picker demonstrate how to extract the meat from a crab.

For persons not lucky enough to have a "picky" preceptor, guidance is hereby provided.

Picking blue crabs involves at least eight separate steps. The order of steps varies with different pickers. The following sequence is one method (see photos on the following two pages).

**How to Pick a Crab:**

1) Remove the crab's claws and legs by folding them under the body. Try to leave the meat in the crab's body instead of letting it come off on the claws and legs. If meat does come off on a claw or leg, save the pieces of meat. Save the claws. Discard all the walking legs except one.

2) Use the tip of the remaining walking leg (a knife can also be used) to loosen the point of the apron on the underside of the crab's shell. Pull off the apron. Discard the apron and last walking leg.

3) Loosen and pull off the top of the shell. Pull up on either the back of the shell (near where a swim paddle attaches) or on the lateral spine of the shell. Discard the top shell.

4) Pull off the grayish gills, also known as dead man's fingers (the gills are not edible, but they are not poisonous as has been rumored).

5) Break off the crab's mouth parts by grasping them between thumb and index finger and pressing down. Discard the mouth parts. Clean out the innards of the crab, located in the channel in the middle of the crab (some save the innards to eat). Rinse with cold water to remove remnants.

6) Break the body in half. Some pickers (especially professional pickers) cut the leg and claw sockets away from the body prior to breaking the body in half. Cutting away the leg and claw sockets makes picking the meat from the body easier.

7) Cut or break each half of the body in half again. Pick the meat out of each body part. This step takes practice! Each picker should just dive in and acquire his/her own style.

8) Break each claw at the joint, leaving two pieces per claw. Using a nutcracker or mallet, crack each piece. Try to pull the meat out in one piece. If unsuccessful, pick out the meat in smaller pieces.

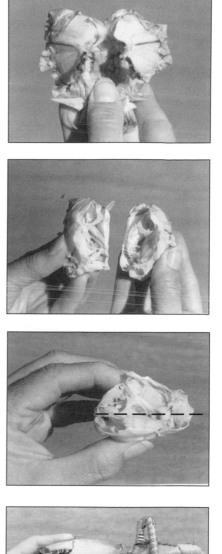

The edible meat of the crab is located inside the two pieces of each claw and the two cartilage-bound compartments on either side of the crab's body.

Meat from the crab's body is tender and white. A good-sized piece of meat, called *lump* or *backfin*, is attached to the swim paddle at the back of the crab's body. This piece is considered by some to be the choicest, easiest-to-extract, meat in the crab.

The meat from the crab's claws is flaky and somewhat darker.

Whether crab meat is from the body or claws, it is very tasty. Claw meat is quite acceptable to use in most recipes.

## Sharing the Crabbing Chores

*Youngsters can pick crabs, too!*

The tasks of catching, cooking, cleaning, and picking crabs entail significant work. Splitting these duties among family members keeps a fun crustacean quest from becoming an arduous crabby crusade.

Splitting the crabbing duties works nicely: One person catches, cooks, and cleans the crabs, getting them ready for picking. Another person assumes the task of picking. Cooking falls to whomever is hungry for a delicious crab meal.

## Alternate Ways to Procure Crab Meat

Fresh, already-cooked-and-picked crab meat can be purchased at many seafood stores.

Packaged crab meat is typically sold in 8, 12, and 16 oz. (1 lb.) plastic containers. The meat is classified and priced by several criteria:

**Lump** or **jumbo lump** meat contains large, white pieces of meat from the back of the crab's body, the area that moves the swim paddles. Lump is generally the most expensive meat.

**Backfin** includes lump and larger flakes from the crab's body. It should contain very few pieces of shell. Backfin is generally more expensive than claw meat.

**Special** or **flake** is smaller flakes of white, body meat other than lump. This meat comes from the anterior parts of the crab's body, parts that move the crab's walking legs. More pieces of shell are typically found in this meat than in lump meat, because the front of the crab's body is harder to pick.

**Deluxe** is a combination of all the meat from the crab's body.

**Claw** contains the darker, flaky meat from the crab's claws. Claw is generally less expensive, yet still quite tasty.

Crab meat is also available frozen and canned. Though fresh crab meat is definitely preferred tastewise, frozen or canned meat has the advantage of being available at times when fresh crab is not. Canned meat is pasteurized (cooked thoroughly to kill all germs).

Be aware of *imitation* crab meat products. Imitation crab is made from processed fish, to which crab flavoring has been added. The appearance and consistency of imitation crab is decent, but it simply cannot match the taste of real crab.

## Using Crab Meat

A good-sized crab supplies about ¼ cup of crab meat; four crabs provide one cup of meat. One crab contains 1 to 2 oz. of meat, depending on its size and whether it still has two claws. About 10 to 14 crabs are needed to make a pound (16 oz.) of fresh crab meat; 5 to 7 crabs will furnish a half pound (8 oz.) of meat.

Fresh-picked crab meat should be used as soon as possible. It will keep for three or four days in the coldest section of the refrigerator, if needed.

Crab meat should be "repicked" before adding the meat to a recipe. No matter how carefully crabs are initially picked, a few pieces of cartilage or shell invariably remain in the meat. These bits of cartilage can be removed by kneading crab meat through one's fingertips a few pieces at a time.

## Freezing Crab Meat

Some sources state crab meat cannot be frozen. Not true!

Crabs can be frozen several ways: 1) uncooked and whole, 2) cooked and whole, 3) cleaned and uncooked (claws and bodies), 4) cleaned and cooked (claws and bodies), or 5) already cooked-and-picked meat, frozen in water or milk.

Freezing already cooked-and-picked crab in water or milk works well. Place the meat in a freezer container. Pour in milk or water to just cover the meat. Label the container as to contents, amount, and date frozen.

To utilize crab frozen in water or milk, thaw the container overnight in the refrigerator, or by placing the container in cold water for an hour or two. Do not thaw the meat slowly at room temperature, because bacteria can multiply.

Crab frozen in milk or water is spongier in texture than fresh crab. The taste, however, is quite acceptable.

Another way to savor crab in the cold, off-season is to freeze recipes containing crab. Make a double portion of crab spaghetti, crab chowder, or crab gumbo, and store the uneaten portion in the freezer.

Soft-shell crabs can be frozen uncooked, either cleaned or uncleaned.

Never refreeze crabs or crab meat once they are thawed.

# Eat 'em!
## Blue Crab Recipes

## Fresh Seafood is:
* Good for you — provides healthy eating.
* High in protein.
* Low in fat, saturated fat, and calories.
* Contains omega-3 fatty acids (heart healthy).
* Low in salt.
* Full of essential vitamins and minerals.
* An excellent alternative to red meat.
* Available in a wide variety of types and flavors.
* Pleasing to the palate (tastes great).

Seafood is, without doubt, both healthy and tasty. The American Heart Association recommends two to three meals of fish per week for prevention of heart disease.

Why, then, do so many seafood restaurants insist on deep-frying seafood or adding unnecessary high-fat ingredients to seafood recipes? Frying or adding heavy, fatty ingredients not only erodes the nutritional value of seafood, but also it blunts the taste of delicacies from the sea.

Instead, seafood should be prepared in a manner that retains its healthy nourishment and tantalizing taste.

---

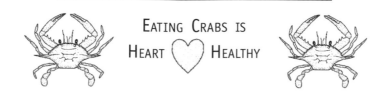

EATING CRABS IS
HEART ♡ HEALTHY

## Nutrition – Blue Crab Meat

Crab meat is delicious and nutritious. Like most seafood, crab is high in protein, vitamins, and minerals. Only 16 percent of the calories in blue crab meat are from fat. Saturated fat (the main culprit in raising blood cholesterol levels) is very low. In addition, crab meat contains small amounts of omega-3 fatty acids, which might be heart-protective.

A soft-shell crab, eaten whole (shell and all), is high in calcium.

Three ounces of blue crab meat (two large crabs or three small crabs) supply 87 calories.

| 3 oz. crabmeat | 3 oz. "lean" ground beef |
|---|---|
| 87 total calories | 230 total calories |
| 14 calories from fat | 144 calories from fat |
| 16% calories from fat | 63% calories from fat |
| total fat 1.5 grams | total fat 16 grams |
| saturated fat 0.2 grams | saturated fat 6.2 grams |
| protein 17 grams | protein 21 grams |
| carbohydrate 0 grams | carbohydrate 0 grams |
| cholesterol 85 mg. | cholesterol 74 mg. |
| sodium 237 mg. | sodium 39 mg. |

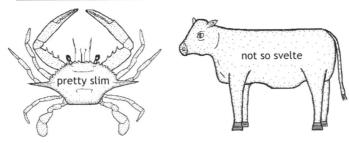

pretty slim

not so svelte

## Crab Recipes

Recipes for seafood dishes can and should be healthy. The following recipes are tasty, and low, or at least reduced, in fat.

*Cold crab dips are a great way to enjoy crab in warm weather.*

### CREAM CHEESE CRAB DIP

8 oz. light (reduced fat), soft cream cheese
1 Tbs. ketchup
$1/4$ tsp. Worcestershire sauce
$1/4$ tsp. red cayenne pepper
$1/8$ tsp. black pepper
4 sprinkles hot pepper sauce
8 oz. crab meat (can substitute shrimp or squid, diced)

Sift crab meat through fingertips to remove any shell fragments. Mix all ingredients together. Cover and store in the refrigerator. Serve on Ritz or other crackers.

### CREAMY CRAB DIP

4 oz. low-fat, plain yogurt
4 oz. light (reduced fat), soft cream cheese
$1/2$ Tbs. green onion, chopped fine
2 tsp. fresh parsley, minced (or 1 tsp. dried)
$1/2$ Tbs. lemon juice
$1/2$ tsp. mustard
$1/2$ tsp. horseradish
$1/4$ tsp. dill weed
6 to 8 oz. fresh crab meat

Sift crab meat through fingertips to remove any shell fragments. Combine all ingredients, except crab, in a bowl. Mix well. Stir in crab. Cover and store in the refrigerator. Serve on Ritz or melba toast crackers.

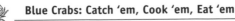 

*Hot crab dip is par excellence — a great way to start any meal.*

## HOT CRAB DIP

8 oz. fresh crab meat
4 oz. light (reduced fat), brick cream cheese
$1/4$ cup fat-free sour cream
1 tsp. horseradish
1 Tbs. mayonnaise
1 tsp. Worcestershire sauce
$1/4$ tsp. dried mustard
2 Tbs. milk
$3/4$ tsp. fresh lemon juice
1 to 2 oz. cheddar cheese, shredded
Paprika

Allow cream cheese to soften in a bowl. Sift crab meat through fingertips to remove any shell fragments. Combine all ingredients except crab, half of cheddar cheese, and paprika in a bowl. Mix well. Fold in crab. Transfer mixture to a small baking dish. Sprinkle remaining cheese and paprika on top. Bake at 350° for 20 minutes or until bubbly on the outside. Serve on Ritz, melba toast, or whole wheat crackers.

Note: Cutting the recipe in half for a smaller amount of hot crab dip works fine.

## CRAB SALAD DABS

6 to 7 oz. crab meat
1 Tbs. onion, chopped fine
1 Tbs. green pepper, chopped fine
$1/4$ cup celery, chopped fine
1 Tbs. fresh parsley, chopped fine (1 tsp. dried)
1 tsp. fresh lime juice (or lemon juice)
$1/8$ tsp. white pepper
4 sprinkles hot pepper sauce
3 Tbs. fat-free mayonnaise
Hot green pepper sauce

Sift crab meat through fingertips to remove any shell pieces. Mix all ingredients gently. Store in refrigerator for later use.

Serve with crackers. Spoon a dab of crab mixture onto a cracker. Place a drop of green hot sauce on top of each crab dab.

## CRAB SALAD

10 oz. fresh crab meat
$1/2$ cup celery, chopped fine
$1/3$ cup red onion, chopped fine
$1/4$ cup fat-free mayonnaise
$1 1/2$ Tbs. fresh parsley, chopped fine ($1/2$ Tbs. dried)
2 tsp. fresh tarragon, chopped (1 tsp. dried)
2 tsp. fresh lime juice
$1/8$ tsp. white pepper
$1/8$ tsp. hot pepper sauce
Lettuce or crackers
Hot green pepper sauce

Sift crab meat through fingertips to remove any shell fragments. Gently mix all ingredients except lettuce, crackers, and green pepper sauce. Store in refrigerator, chilling for later use.

Serve on lettuce or with crackers. Spoon a dab of crab mixture onto a cracker. Put one drop of green hot sauce on top.

## CRAB FINGERS

*Crab "fingers"— a simple but elegant way to enjoy the excellent taste of blue crab claw meat.*

Crab claws
$1/4$ cup ketchup
1 Tbs. horseradish
$1/2$ tsp. fresh lemon juice

Remove the meat from crab claws, leaving the meat intact, in whole pieces, as much as possible.

Combine ketchup, horseradish, and lemon to make a cocktail sauce. Using a small fork, spear the crab fingers, dip them in the cocktail sauce, and pop them into your mouth.

Voila! Instant crab delight.

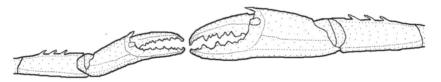

*Crab claw meat is finger-licking good!*

## CRAB FEAST

*A crab feast is a festive occasion: a celebration of the bounty of the sea. Gather friends and family, and make a party of the event.*

Boil or steam a mess of crabs right where the crab feast is held. A good location is outdoors or on a screened-in porch — the smell of cooking crabs and the mess of cracking and picking crabs is not a problem.

Cover a picnic table with newspaper or brown paper. Have plenty of cold drinks on hand. Nutcrackers or mallets, along with short knives and other picking tools, are helpful.

As soon as the crabs are cooked, pile the red-shelled delectables on the table. Pick and eat the crabs promptly. Enjoy table talk and a favorite beverage while partaking of the crustacean bounty.

A crab feast is a messy affair. Pieces of shell or crab juice often end up on people and the floor. Crab remains pile up on the paper-covered table.

After the feast, return leftover crab parts to the sound for consumption by scavengers (but please, make sure no trash goes in the water).

If recycling the crab remnants is impossible, roll the whole mess up in the newspaper and place it in the garbage. Be aware: If leftover crab parts sit in a garbage can for more than a day, they will develop a powerful odor. Sprinkling laundry detergent over the crab remains before disposal helps to minimize the odor.

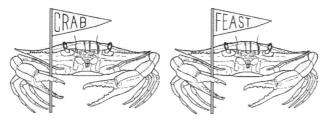

## CRAB PINEAPPLE DELIGHT

*Crab pineapple is a low-fat recipe. The dish can be used as an appetizer or as the main course of a meal. The combination of crab and pineapple is a taste-pleaser.*

1 1/2 to 2 cups crab meat
1/4 cup fat-free mayonnaise
1/2 tsp. Worcestershire sauce
3 to 4 drops hot pepper sauce
1 can (15 oz.) pineapple chunks or rings
1 cup corn flakes
Paprika

Sift crab meat through fingertips to remove any remaining shell fragments. Combine crab meat, mayonnaise, Worcestershire sauce, and hot pepper sauce. Mix gently.

Place corn flakes in a large baggie; crush flakes fine. Add pineapple pieces several at a time, shaking to coat them. Place 6 to 10 pineapple pieces (or one pineapple ring) in individual casserole dishes. Top with crab mixture. Scatter leftover crumbs on top. Sprinkle lightly with paprika. Bake at 350° for 20 to 25 minutes, until crumbs are lightly browned. Serves four to five.

+ = Yum

## CRAB SOUP

*Quick, yet elegant and rich tasting.*

1 can (11 oz.) condensed tomato soup
1 can (11 oz.) condensed split pea soup
2% milk (11 oz.)
$^1$/4 cup evaporated milk
1 cup fresh crab meat
$^1$/4 cup dry sherry (optional)

Sift crab meat through fingertips to remove hidden shell fragments. Blend soups and milk in a pot, then cook on low to medium heat until warm (do not boil). Add crab meat.

Add sherry if desired. Sherry adds a rich taste to the soup. Serves four.

## CRAB SANDWICHES

*Simple, yet tasty. Enjoy!*

Fresh crab meat
Fresh sandwich buns/bread
Low-fat mozzarella cheese
Tomato
Lettuce or alfalfa sprouts

Sift crab meat through fingertips to remove hidden shell fragments. Spread a layer of crab meat on the bun. Place a thin slice of cheese on top of the crab meat. Broil to melt the cheese and warm the crab and bread. Place a slice of tomato and lettuce or sprouts over the melted cheese.

Optional: Toast the bread/bun first.

## CRAB-CLAM RED CHOWDER

1 carrot
1 celery stalk
1 small onion
$1/4$ cup green pepper
8 oz. baby corn
1 can (15 oz.) diced tomatoes, undrained
1 can (15 oz.) fat-free chicken broth
6 Tbs. clam juice
$1/4$ tsp. dried thyme
$1/8$ tsp. freshly-ground black pepper
3 dashes hot pepper sauce
$2^{1}/2$ oz. orzo
8 medium clams, chopped
2 to 4 oz. fresh crab meat

Chop vegetables into small pieces. Combine vegetables (include juice of tomatoes), spices, clam juice, and broth in a pot. Bring to a boil, reduce heat, then simmer 5 minutes. Add orzo, and simmer 10 more minutes. Add clams and cook another 5 minutes. Pick through crab meat to remove any shell fragments, then stir in crab meat prior to serving. Serves four.

*Hot pepper sauce, a welcome addition to many seafood recipes.*

## CRAB-CLAM NEW ENGLAND CHOWDER

1 small to medium onion
1 large carrot
1 stalk celery
1$^1$/$_2$ Tbs. margarine
1 large potato
1$^1$/$_2$ Tbs. flour
2$^1$/$_2$ cups 2% milk
$^1$/$_2$ cup clam liquid
$^1$/$_8$ to $^1$/$_4$ cup white wine
$^1$/$_4$ tsp. white pepper
$^1$/$_2$ tsp. dried thyme
3 to 5 dashes hot pepper sauce
6 to 8 medium clams, chopped (or 6 $^1$/$_2$ oz. can)
1 chicken breast, skinned, deboned, and chopped
$^1$/$_2$ to 1 cup fresh crab meat
Optional: shrimp or fish

Chop vegetables into small pieces. Sauté onion, celery, carrot, and chicken in margarine for a few minutes. Mix flour into $^3$/$_4$ cup milk, add the rest of the milk, then pour mixture slowly over sautéed vegetables and chicken. Add potato, clam liquid, wine, spices, and hot sauce. Bring to a gentle boil, reduce heat, and simmer 20 to 30 minutes. Add clams. Five minutes later add crab (fish/shrimp), and cook another 3 to 5 minutes.

Serves four.

Note: Oysters, mussels, fish, shrimp, or virtually any seafood can be used in this recipe.

*The chef can enjoy a little wine while
preparing seafood recipes.*

## CRAB AND CORN CHOWDER

*A great way to enjoy the taste of fresh corn and crab in the spring.*

4 ears fresh corn (or 3 cups frozen)
$3/4$ Tbs. margarine
$1/2$ cup onion (1 small onion)
$1/4$ cup green pepper
$1/3$ cup celery
2 Tbs. green onions, chopped fine
1 cup fat-free chicken broth
$1^1/2$ cups (12 oz.) evaporated skim milk
$1/4$ tsp. white pepper
$1/4$ tsp. salt
1 cup fresh crab meat
Black pepper

Cut the corn kernels from the corn cobs. Blend corn kernels in a food processor until creamy in consistency. Set aside.

Chop vegetables into very small pieces. In a large pot, sauté onion, green pepper, and celery in margarine for 2 to 3 minutes. Add corn, milk, and spices. Reduce heat to low and cook for 20 to 25 minutes, stirring frequently. Add crab, cook on low for an additional 5 minutes. Add black pepper to taste at the table.

Serves four.

Option: Substitute shrimp or crawfish for crab.

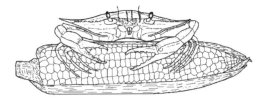

## CRAB OMELET

*A delightfully delectable breakfast. Just one crab will provide ample crab meat for this meal.*

3 to 4 eggs
$^1/4$ cup low-fat milk
Black pepper to taste
Dash of nutmeg (one shake)
Non-stick spray
Fillings: vegetables such as green pepper, mushrooms, tomato,
    alfalfa sprouts, celery, green onion, etc.
1 to 2 oz. fresh crab meat (1 crab will suffice)
1 to 2 oz. low-fat cheddar cheese, shredded
Picante sauce

Combine eggs, milk, pepper, and nutmeg in a bowl; stir together. Chop vegetables into small pieces. Spray a medium to large skillet with non-stick cooking spray. Pre-heat the skillet over medium to high heat. Pour the egg mixture into the skillet. Let the mixture cook slowly until the egg mixture is not runny, adjusting the heat downward so the underside does not burn. Add the crab, vegetables, and cheese onto one half of the omelet, then fold the other half over on top. Cook another few minutes to melt the cheese and cook the vegetables lightly. Spoon picante sauce on top of the omelet servings at the table.

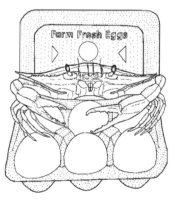

Serves two to three.

## CRAB CAKES

*Crab cakes are typically fried, and the ingredients used sometimes render the cakes high in fat.*

*The following recipes are delicious, low-fat versions of crab cakes. Broiling the cakes, instead of frying, subtracts fat, not flavor.*

*The key to tasty crab cakes is being generous with the crab meat and easy with other ingredients.*

## CRAB CAKES I

Meat from 10 to 12 crabs ($2^1/2$ to 3 cups or 1 pound)
20 Ritz crackers
1 Tbs. Worcestershire sauce
2 tsp. chopped, dried parsley (4 tsp. fresh)
$1^1/2$ tsp. mustard
1 Tbs. fat-free mayonnaise
1 egg
$1/4$ tsp. hot pepper sauce
$1/8$ tsp. thyme
Dash of nutmeg (one shake)

Crush crackers fine. Sift through crab meat with fingertips to remove any shell fragments. Mix all ingredients in a bowl. Form mixture into patties. Place patties on broiling platter coated with non-stick cooking spray. Broil patties for 5 to 7 minutes on each side. Serve with cocktail sauce.

Any leftover crab cakes can be served the next day in sandwiches. Use fresh buns; top the patties with cocktail sauce, and lettuce or alfalfa sprouts.

Notes: To lower the fat content even further, use only the egg white, omitting the yolk.

Squid or octopus can be substituted for crab in this recipe or any crab cake recipe.

## CRAB CAKES II

Meat from 8 to 12 crabs (2 to 3 cups or $^3/4$ to 1 pound)
$^1/2$ cup dried, herb-seasoned stuffing (a bit more if more crab)
2 small green onions, chopped fine
1$^1/2$ Tbs. chopped, fresh parsley ($^3/4$ Tbs. dried)
2 Tbs. fat-free mayonnaise
6 Tbs. ($^3/8$ cup) 2% milk
$^1/4$ tsp. white pepper
$^1/8$ tsp. hot pepper sauce

Crush stuffing fine. Sift through crab meat to remove any small pieces of shell. Mix all ingredients in a bowl. Form mixture into patties. Put patties on a broiling pan or tray lightly coated with non-stick cooking spray. Refrigerate 20 to 30 minutes or until ready to cook. Broil patties for 5 minutes on each side. Serve with cocktail sauce.

Leftovers can be served the next day for sandwiches, using fresh buns, topped with cocktail sauce, and lettuce or alfalfa sprouts.

## CRAB CAKES III

Meat from 8 to 12 crabs (2 to 3 cups or $^3/4$ to 1 pound)
$^3/4$ cup dried, herb-seasoned stuffing or seasoned bread crumbs
$^1/4$ cup onion, chopped fine
$^1/4$ cup green pepper, chopped fine
$^1/4$ cup fat-free mayonnaise
1 egg white
$^1/4$ tsp. Worcestershire sauce
1 tsp. Old Bay seasoning
1 tsp. dried mustard

Crush stuffing fine. Sift through crab meat to remove any small pieces of shell. Mix all ingredients in a bowl. Refrigerate 30 to 60 minutes. Form into patties. Put patties on broiling pan lightly coated with non-stick cooking spray. Broil patties for 4 to 5 minutes on each side. Serve with cocktail sauce.

# CRAB SPAGHETTI

*Crab spaghetti is a wonderful, easy-to-fix dish that will delight diners' taste buds. The unique taste of this recipe is a refreshing change from other marinara (red sauce over pasta) recipes.*

*Crab spaghetti freezes well. It provides a delicious crab meal in the winter, when crabs are not available.*

Meat from four blue crabs (1 cup)
$^{1}/_{2}$ cup chopped celery
$^{1}/_{2}$ cup chopped onion (1 small onion)
1 Tbs. dried parsley flakes (2 Tbs. fresh)
$^{1}/_{2}$ clove garlic, pressed or chopped fine
8 oz. can tomato sauce
16 oz. can chopped tomatoes, drained
$^{1}/_{2}$ tsp. paprika
$^{1}/_{8}$ tsp. black pepper
12 oz. spaghetti
1 Tbs. butter

Sauté celery, onion, parsley, and garlic in butter until tender (a few minutes). Add tomato sauce, tomatoes, and spices. Simmer for 20 minutes, stirring occasionally. Cook spaghetti in a separate pot during the last 10 minutes that the sauce is cooking. While the spaghetti and sauce cook, sift through the crab meat to remove any small pieces of shell. Fold the crab meat into the sauce and cook just a few more minutes to heat the crab meat. Ladle moderate amounts of sauce over the pasta. Sprinkle with parmesan cheese if desired.

Serves four.

Note: Don't add too much crab meat. More is not better in this recipe.

Note: Sauté with water or wine (not butter) to further decrease fat calories.

## CRAB TOSTADAS

1 medium onion, chopped
$^1/_2$ Tbs. margarine
1 can (16 oz.) fat-free refried beans
Taco seasoning packet ($1^1/_4$ oz.)
Toppings: chopped vegetables such as celery, carrots, green
    pepper, banana pepper rings, tomato, lettuce, alfalfa sprouts
Tostada shells
6 oz. fresh crab meat
6 oz. low-fat cheddar cheese, shredded
Picante sauce and/or green taco sauce

In a medium to large skillet, sauté onion for a few minutes in
margarine. Add refried beans and taco seasoning, 2 to 3 oz.
water, then cook for another 10 to 15 minutes. Chop vegetable
toppings. Spread tostada shells on a cookie sheet, and bake at
325° for 5 minutes. Sift through crab meat with fingertips to
remove any remaining shell parts. Stir crab meat into beans and
simmer 3 minutes. Spoon crab-bean mix onto tostada shells,
sprinkle cheese on top, and bake another few minutes to melt the
cheese. Add toppings and taco sauce at the table.
    Note: To decrease fat even further, sauté onion in water.

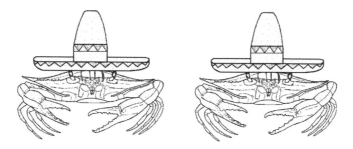

## DEVILED CRAB

1 can (11 oz.) low-fat cream of celery soup
1¹/₄ to 1¹/₂ cups fresh crab meat
1 Tbs. onion, chopped
2 Tbs. green pepper, chopped
3 Tbs. 2% milk
1 tsp. lemon juice
1 tsp. Worcestershire sauce
¹/₂ tsp. mustard
¹/₄ tsp. hot pepper sauce
2 to 3 Tbs. bread crumbs
Paprika

Sift crab meat with fingertips to remove any shell fragments.

Gently mix all ingredients, except paprika and bread crumbs, in a bowl. Transfer to an ungreased baking dish (or individual, small dishes). Sprinkle with bread crumbs, then shake paprika on top of the mixture. Bake 20 to 25 minutes at 350° until the edges are bubbling and the top is lightly browned.

Makes four small servings.

Note: Double the recipe to make enough to use this dish as a main course.

## Seafood Gumbo

$^{1}/_{2}$ pound fish fillets, chopped in bite-size pieces
$^{1}/_{2}$ pound raw shrimp, peeled, chopped in bite-size pieces
3 to 4 oz. fresh crab meat (3 crabs, picked)
2 Tbs. butter
1 cup celery, chopped
$^{3}/_{4}$ cup green onions, chopped
$^{1}/_{2}$ cup green pepper, chopped
$1^{1}/_{2}$ Tbs. fresh parsley, chopped
1 clove garlic, minced
1 Tbs. all-purpose flour
1 tsp. chili powder
1 tsp. paprika
$^{1}/_{8}$ tsp. red cayenne pepper
$^{1}/_{8}$ tsp. salt
1 can (8 oz.) tomato sauce
$^{1}/_{2}$ cup fat-free chicken broth
1 can (14.5 oz.) chopped tomatoes, drained
6 oz. okra, fresh or frozen
6 cups cooked rice
Hot pepper sauce

Sauté garlic, onion, celery, green pepper, and parsley in butter a few minutes. Mix flour, paprika, chili powder, cayenne, and salt, then stir mixture into vegetables. Add tomato sauce, chicken broth, and tomatoes. Bring to a boil, then reduce heat. Simmer 12 to 15 minutes, stirring occasionally.

Sift crab meat with fingertips to remove any shell fragments.

Add okra and simmer for 4 minutes, then add seafood and simmer for 5 more minutes. Serve over rice. Add hot sauce to taste at the table.

Tips: Virtually any seafood can be utilized in this recipe. Use whatever is available. If preferred, the vegetables can be sautéed in water or wine to further reduce fat content.

## CRAB AND SHRIMP JAMBALAYA

$^1/_2$ cup onion, chopped fine
$^1/_4$ cup green pepper, chopped fine
$^1/_3$ cup celery, chopped fine
$1^1/_2$ Tbs. fresh parsley, chopped fine
1 Tbs. margarine
$1^1/_2$ cups (12 oz.) fat-free chicken broth
$^1/_4$ tsp. red cayenne pepper
$^1/_4$ tsp. fresh-ground black pepper
$^1/_8$ tsp. white pepper
$^1/_2$ tsp. dried oregano
1 cup raw shrimp, peeled and chopped
$^1/_4$ cup (3 small) green onions, chopped fine
1 cup fresh crab meat
2 cups cooked rice

In a medium pan, melt butter. Sauté onion, green pepper, celery, and parsley a few minutes. Add the spices and chicken broth, and bring to a boil. Then reduce heat and cook on low for 10 minutes. Add shrimp and cook another 3 minutes. Add green onions, crab, and rice, then cook just another minute or two until heated thoroughly. Cover and let stand 5 minutes before serving.

Serves three to four.

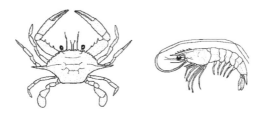

## CRAB NEW ORLEANS

10 to 12 oz. fresh crab meat
1 can (11 oz.) cream of celery soup
1 cup fresh or frozen peas
1 cup fresh or frozen corn
1 can (7 oz.) mushroom pieces, undrained
1/8 tsp. black pepper
Herb-seasoned stuffing (dried, seasoned bread crumbs)
Hot pepper sauce

Preheat oven to 350°. Combine soup, vegetables, and pepper in a lightly-greased baking dish. Sift crab meat with fingertips to remove any shell fragments. Fold crab meat into mixture. Top with stuffing/bread crumbs. Bake 40 to 50 minutes (10 minutes longer if using frozen vegetables) until casserole is bubbling around the edges. Add hot sauce to taste at the table. Serves four.

## CRAB CASSEROLE

1 small onion, chopped fine
3 Tbs. green pepper, chopped fine
2 Tbs. margarine
2 cups 2% milk
3 Tbs. flour
4 oz. light cream cheese (brick, not soft tub)
2 cups fresh crab meat
$2/3$ cup cheddar cheese, shredded
$2/3$ cup herb-seasoned stuffing (dried, seasoned bread crumbs)
Dash of nutmeg

Preheat oven to 350°. Sauté onion and green pepper in margarine a few minutes. Stir flour into milk, then add to onion/pepper. Heat and stir until thick and bubbly. Add cream cheese and nutmeg, stir until cheese melts. Add crab meat. Pour into a two quart casserole dish. Sprinkle with cheddar cheese. Top with herb-seasoned stuffing crumbs. Bake 30 to 45 minutes or until casserole is bubbly and topping is browned. Serves four to five.

*Just a pinch (one shake) of nutmeg is an excellent addition to many crab recipes.*

## CRAB-CHEESE CASSEROLE

1 1/2 cups fresh crab meat
1/2 cup celery, chopped fine
1/2 cup green onion, chopped fine
1/3 cup green pepper, chopped fine
1 1/2 cups toasted bread, cut into cubes
1 cup low-fat cottage cheese
1/2 cup part skim mozzarella cheese, shredded
2 Tbs. fat-free mayonnaise
2 tsp. fresh lemon juice
1 tsp. Worcestershire sauce
1/8 tsp. hot pepper sauce
Paprika

Preheat oven to 350°. Combine all ingredients except paprika
in a large bowl and mix gently. Scoop into a 1 1/2 to 2 quart,
lightly-greased casserole dish. Sprinkle paprika on top. Bake 30
minutes. Serves four.

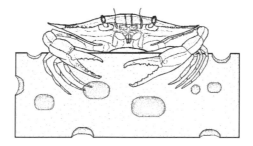

## STUFFED FLOUNDER

Flounder fillets, top-side skinned, bottom scaled
Crab meat, 6 to 8 oz. (3 to 5 crabs)
$^1/_2$ stalk celery, chopped fine
2 green onions, chopped fine
3 to 4 mushrooms, chopped fine
12 saltine crackers, crushed
$1^1/_2$ Tbs. butter, melted
Black pepper
Paprika
1 dash of nutmeg (one shake)
1 Tbs. fresh parsley, chopped fine
Sauce: $1^1/_2$ Tbs. butter
$^1/_3$ lemon, squeezed into butter

Preheat oven to 350°. Rinse and dry flounder fillets. Spray a baking dish with non-stick cooking spray. Arrange half the fillets in the bottom of the dish, skin-side down. Sprinkle with black pepper and paprika.

Combine crab meat with the other ingredients and mix together. Place the crab stuffing on the bottom fillets, then cover with the top fillets. Pour sauce over top. Bake for 20 minutes. Test to make sure fish is done (fish will flake easily). Serve at once. Makes four servings.

Note: Other fish can be substituted for flounder.

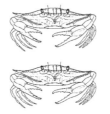
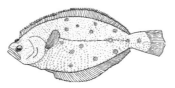

# All About Blue Crabs

## Crustaceans/Crabs

Everyone knows what a crab is — a hard-shelled animal with pincers. But, is a blue crab a "true crab"? Is a blue crab a crustacean, too?

Scientists use the terms *crab*, *true crab*, and *crustacean* to mean different things. The organization of crab-like animals into related groups is somewhat confusing, but can be understood as follows (see diagram below):

Crabs and crustaceans belong to the phylum Arthropoda. Arthropods are invertebrate animals (no backbone), with segmented bodies, jointed legs, and a hard exoskeleton (outer shell). They are the most numerous and widespread group of animals on earth, numbering nearly a million species. Seventy-five percent of *all* animals on earth are arthropods. They occupy almost every environmental niche possible.

Land arthropods include insects, spiders, mites, scorpions, millipedes, and centipedes. Marine arthropods include the horseshoe crab, sea spiders, and crustaceans.

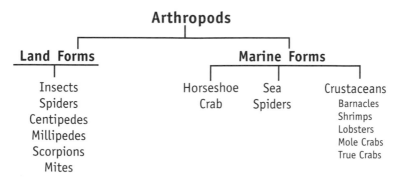

*Crustaceans are the marine equivalent of insects, spiders, scorpions, et al.*

The horseshoe crab is unique enough to be classified by itself. Technically, it is neither crab nor crustacean.

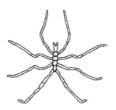

Sea spiders are tiny ($^1/_{16}$ to $^1/_2$ inch) animals that resemble land spiders. Though common, sea spiders are inconspicuous, blending into heavy growths of plants and animals on rocks and pilings.

Crustaceans include barnacles, mole crabs, hermit crabs, true crabs, shrimps, krill, and lobsters. Barnacles, though they resemble mollusks, are actually sessile (permanently fixed in place) crustaceans. Mole crabs, hermit crabs, shrimps, krill, and lobsters are classified separately from true crabs by subtle differences in body form and leg location.

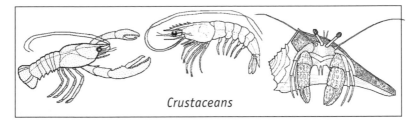

*Crustaceans*

True crabs include species such as blue, fiddler, ghost, marsh, oyster, and stone crabs. True crabs are crustaceans with short tails folded under the body and a front pair of legs modified into pincers.

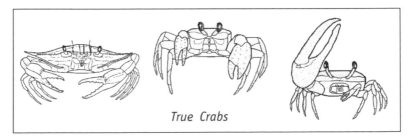

*True Crabs*

If the classification of crabs and crustaceans is still confusing, do not despair: Think of crustaceans as creatures occupying marine niches corresponding to terrestrial niches of their land relatives; in other words, *crustaceans are the marine equivalent of insects, spiders, scorpions, et al.* Marine arthropods grow bigger because water helps support the weight of their shell; land arthropods are limited in size by the weight of their exoskeleton.

insect of the land

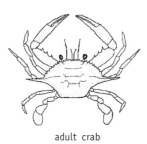

insect of the sea

*"Insects of the sea" is an apt description of blue crabs. Like insects, blue crabs have an external shell, jointed appendages, segmented bodies, and they molt to grow. Blue crabs grow larger than land-based insects because their weight is supported by buoyant water.*

Most crustaceans undergo metamorphosis during their early development. Metamorphosis is the distinct change in body form an animal undergoes developing from an embryo to an adult. Early forms often do not resemble adult animals.

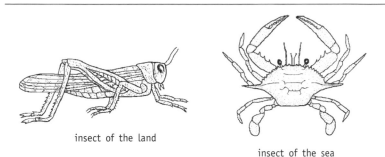

first larval stage          second larval stage                    adult crab

*Metamorphosis in a blue crab.*

71

Molting is another process common to crustaceans (and many land arthropods, too). An external skeleton provides excellent protection. In order to grow, however, a crustacean must periodically shed its external shell. Although the new shell hardens in a few days time, a newly-molted crustacean is vulnerable to predators until its shell is hard.

Crustaceans share an unusual defense mechanism. They are able to sacrifice one or more of their own legs in order to escape from a predator. If a predator grabs hold of a crab's leg, the predator may pull the leg off, or the crab may break off its own leg and flee. This process, called autotomy, sacrifices a limb in order to save the crab's life. The limb breaks off at a specific joint specially adapted not to bleed if the limb is severed. The crab (or other crustacean) regrows the lost limb at later molts, though it may take three to four molts for the limb to attain full size.

## True Crabs

The hallmark of true crabs is an abdomen curled under the body. Five pairs of legs are present; the first pair of legs is modified into claws, which are used in feeding, defense, and display. The upper body shell (carapace) is typically broad, and expanded on both sides to cover the gills.

About 4,500 species of true crabs have been identified. Not surprisingly, crab species vary greatly in color, size, and habitat.

Body colors in crabs range from the pale, translucent white of an oyster crab (which lives in oysters, mussels, and other bivalves), to the olive-green of a blue crab, to the brilliant red of a scarlet crab.

Sizewise, crabs range from less than 1/4 inch wide (male oyster crabs) to 15 feet in width (the giant spider crab of Japan).

Crabs are largely marine creatures. Most species inhabit shallow, coastal waters, but some species live in hydrothermal vents, miles below the ocean's surface. Only a few species live on land or in fresh water.

The claws of crabs vary greatly in size and shape among species. Claw size and shape can even vary in one individual species. For example, in the male fiddler crab, one claw is dramatically larger than the other claw.

Most crabs have four pairs of walking legs, and move about mainly by crawling, most often sideways. These crabs typically swim poorly. The blue crab and other swimming crabs have the last pair of legs modified into wide, flat, swimming paddles. This modification enables them to swim quite well.

The abdomen of true crabs, which is folded under the body (unlike the abdomen in other crustaceans), is shaped differently in males and females. Male crabs usually have a narrow abdomen (apron), comprised of a thin strip. Female crabs exhibit a wide abdomen, often encompassing the whole width between the legs.

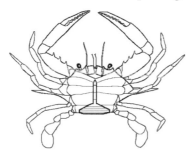 

*Male crab with narrow apron (abdomen) on the underside.*    *Female crab with wide apron (abdomen) on the underside.*

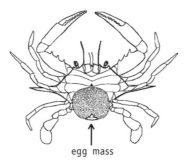

egg mass

Female crabs, with the exception of land crabs, carry their eggs on the abdomen until the eggs hatch. The eggs are thus protected by the female prior to the larvae emerging. The tiny hatchlings look vastly different from adult crabs

Many crabs are eaten by humans. Blue crabs, calico crabs, ghost crabs, rock crabs, stone crabs, green crabs, hermit crabs, and oyster crabs are but a few common crabs that are edible.

# Blue Crabs

| Classification of the Blue Crab | |
|---|---|
| Kingdom | Animalia |
| Phylum | Arthropoda (jointed appendages) |
| Class | Crustacea (having a crust or shell) |
| Order | Decapoda (ten-legged) |
| Family | Portunidae (swimming crabs) |
| Genus | Callinectes (beautiful swimmer) |
| Species | sapidus (tasty or savory) |

*In other words: The beautiful, swimming, blue crab is a ten-legged, jointed, hard-shelled animal that is mighty tasty.*

---

The blue crab, *Callinectes sapidus*, is the common edible crab of the Atlantic Coast. Blue crabs are common in brackish water from Cape Cod, Massachusetts, to Florida, and around to Texas in the Gulf of Mexico. Their range (diagram opposite page) actually extends from Canada (Nova Scotia) to Uruguay, in South America.

Blue crabs have been introduced into other parts of the world, including Europe, the Mediterranean Sea, North Africa, Japan, Southwest Asia, and the West Coast of the United States. Scientists believe that this expansion of the blue crab's range has resulted from flushing of ships' ballasts in these waters.

Other species of blue crab (same genus *Callinectes*, but different species), inhabit the West Coast of the Americas, from California to Peru.

Blue crabs are commonly found in shallow water, less than 100 feet deep, although they have been found at depths of almost 300 feet.

*Range of the blue crab,* Callinectes sapidus. *The blue crab lives in brackish water, down to 100 feet deep, along the eastern coast of North and South America.*

The blue crab's scientific name aptly describes the animal. *Callinectes* is Greek for beautiful swimmer, while *sapidus* is Latin for tasty or savory. Thus, *Callinectes sapidus* means "beautiful, savory swimmer."

Delicious white meat makes the blue crab the object of amateur and professional crabber alike.

## External Anatomy/Appearance

"Green crab" might be a better name for this species: The crab's color is largely olive-green. *Blue* stems from beautiful blue coloration on the crab's claws and legs. Large males (jimmies) usually have the most brilliant blue claws and legs. The tips of the claws and body spines of the blue crab are usually red; the underside of the crab is white.

Like all true crabs, the blue crab has ten legs (five pairs). The first pair of legs is modified into pincers (claws). The next three pairs are walking legs, and the last pair is modified into swim paddles.

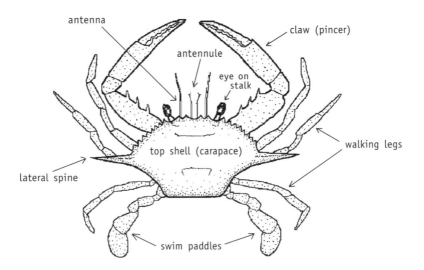

*External anatomy of a blue crab, dorsal (top) view.*

The crab's shell forms a hard, outer layer, protecting its internal organs and muscles. Like the shell of other crustaceans and the outer skin of insects, the blue crab's shell is composed mostly of chitin (the same type material as human fingernails).

The shell of a blue crab is more than twice as wide as it is long. The top part of the crab's shell is called the carapace. Each side of the carapace ends in a long, sharp point, called the lateral spine. The front of the shell is serrated, with eight points between each lateral spine and eye, and four points between the eyes.

The combination of points, spines, and claws of the blue crab gives it a menacing appearance.

A blue crab's eyes are mounted on the ends of movable stalks. The stalked-eye apparatus gives the crab two advantages: 1) 360-degree vision, and 2) the ability to retract its eyes into grooves on the shell when danger threatens.

The two eyes are compound eyes, made up of many separate simple eyes. The eyes provide the crab with a mosaic image, enabling the crab to sense movement of other animals in its environment.

The male blue crab grows a little larger than the female. Differences in claw coloration and apron structure make differentiating male from female crab fairly simple.

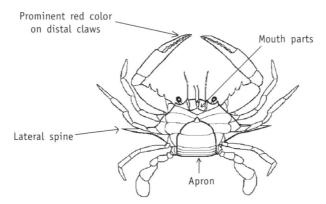

*External anatomy of a female blue crab, underside.*

Red coloration on the claws is more prominent on a female crab; the red is easily seen at a glance (see picture of female crab on the cover). The red coloration on the male's claws is much less evident; only the tips of his claws are red. An easy way to remember this difference: Think of the female crab painting her claws bright red, like a human female painting her nails.

A male crab has a sharply-pointed apron on the bottom of his shell (diagram page 73, picture next page). The female has a rounded apron on her underside. An easy way to visualize the difference: The male's apron resembles the Washington Monument, and the female's apron resembles the Capitol Dome. A juvenile female sports a triangular apron. The pregnant female crab carries a mass of orange eggs on her underside; she is said to be *in sponge*, as the egg mass resembles a sponge.

The claws of a male crab are generally larger than the claws of a comparably-sized female crab.

The two claws of each crab have different sizes and functions. One claw is slightly larger and has knobby (molar-like) teeth; this claw is used for grinding and crushing. The smaller claw has sharper (incisor-like) teeth; it is used for cutting and ripping.

Interestingly, if the bigger, crushing claw is labeled the "dominant-hand" claw, crabs show "right-handedness" and "left-handedness" similar to people. About one-third of crabs are lefthanded (compared to 10% of humans being "left-clawed").

Between the crab's eyes are two long antennae and two short antennules, used by the crab to feel and for chemoreception (taste and smell). Movable mouth parts dominate the area below the antennae. Three pairs of accessory mouth parts, along with a pair of jaws, gather and chop food, then funnel the food into the crab's mouth. The mouth is located just underneath the inner mouth parts.

Hair-like setae form a tan fringe on parts of the crab's appendages and body. Setae, like antennae, function as organs of touch and taste.

The biggest blue crab ever documented measured $9^{1}/_{2}$ inches (lateral shell tip to lateral shell tip) and weighed $1^{1}/_{2}$ pounds.

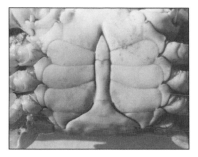

*Apron, male crab.*

*Apron, female crab.*

*Apron, immature female crab.*

*Apron, female sponge crab.*

*Hair-like setae on the walking leg of a blue crab.*

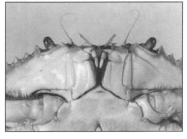

*Mouth parts of a blue crab.*

*Large, crushing claw on the right; small, tearing claw on the left.*

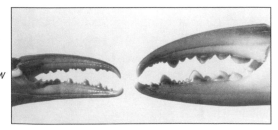

## Internal Anatomy

Much of the internal structure of a blue crab consists of cartilage and muscles. The crab's muscles are connected to the claws, walking legs, and swim paddles, enabling the crab to deftly move these structures. Cartilage serves as rigid attachment for the muscles.

The gills (picture below) of a blue crab are large, prominent structures, consisting of eight filaments on each side of the body.

*Gills and heart of a blue crab.*

Gills enable a crab to breathe water: Oxygen is extracted from water and carbon dioxide is released. The gills also facilitate a blue crab's movements between fresh water and salt water. In response to hormone secretion, more or less salt is allowed to pass through the gills, thereby maintaining the crab's internal salt balance.

The blue crab's heart is a single chamber (a human heart has four chambers) in the middle of the crab's body. Blood flows from the heart to the body to the gills, then back to the heart (no dual circulations, with one to the body and one to the lungs, like humans).

The brain of a blue crab is very small. The brain is located right behind the eyes, in the midline.

*Callinectes sapidus* (the blue crab) is truly a blue-blood among animals. Hemocyanin, a copper-containing chemical in the crab's blood, imparts a blue coloration (similar to iron-containing hemoglobin imparting a red color to human blood).

The stomach of the blue crab is lined with small, hard plates, which finely chop the crab's food (a blue crab has no teeth), thereby aiding digestion.

Although a blue crab has some ability to sense vibrations, it has no true sense of hearing.

## Life Cycle

The life of a blue crab begins when a sperm fertilizes an egg inside a female blue crab. The female places the fertilized egg, along with millions of other eggs, in a spongy mass that she attaches to her abdomen. She carries the egg sponge for two weeks. When the eggs are ready to hatch, the mother releases the hatchlings in an ocean inlet or the ocean itself. Higher water salinity is necessary for hatchling survival.

The life journey of a blue crab begins when it hatches from the egg. The microscopic zoea (pronounced zō-ē-uh) that emerges is just .01 ($^1/_{100}$) inch long (about the size of the period at the end of this sentence). The zoea bears little resemblance to an adult crab. It looks like a tiny, big-eyed, predatory water-mosquito.

The zoea becomes a member of the zooplankton, animals that float in the currents of the open ocean. The zoea is a filter feeder, eating smaller planktonic plants (phytoplankton) and other animals (zooplankton). Growing steadily, the zoea undergoes seven to eight molts over the next six weeks. The final molt results in a dramatic change in body shape: The crab assumes an intermediate megalopa form.

*zoea*

The megalopa, at about 0.1( $^1/_{10}$) inch wide, is large enough to be seen with the naked eye. The megalopa looks more like an adult crab, with two definite claws and four other pairs of legs on its body. A pair of large eyes (megalops means *large eyes*) juts out from the head.

With its two small claws, the megalopa captures other tiny animals to eat.

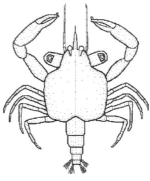

*megalopa*

81

After one to three weeks in the megalopa stage, the megalopa rides ocean currents back into the estuaries and settles on the bottom to live. During its last molt, the megalopa transforms into an adult-shaped animal, a recognizable crab about $^1/_5$ inch in size (measured lateral spine to lateral spine).

In the estuary, the young blue crab grows rapidly, molting every three to five days. The crab reaches one to two inches in size by the time it faces its first winter.

When water temperatures drop below 40°F, a blue crab prepares for a dormant state. In northern waters, the crab hibernates during the winter months. The crab migrates to deeper water, where it digs its back end down into a muddy or sandy bottom. The crab lies buried at a 45° angle. Only the crab's antennae and round eyes on the tips of its eyestalks remain above the mud. Small tunnels in the mud, leading to the crab's gill chambers, are kept open for breathing. The crab ceases growing; molting does not occur. In spring, as the water warms, the crab emerges and returns to shallow water.

The farther south a blue crab lives, the briefer its rest in the mud. In Florida and Gulf Coast waters, a blue crab may not take a mud rest at all. Instead, the crab goes through a period of decreased activity in the colder months.

A small crab matures to adult size in estuaries, undergoing 20 or more molts before it is full-grown. The crab's growth increases with food availability and higher water temperature. Sexual maturity is reached at 12 to 14 months of age.

A male blue crab spends its adult life in the brackish water of sounds and estuaries. A female resides in the same area until her eggs are ready to hatch. She then travels to an inlet or the open ocean and releases her eggs. The life cycle begins again.

On average, only a few of the millions of eggs spawned by a single female reach adulthood. Calculating the age of blue crabs is difficult: With each molt, a crab discards its hard shell, along with any tag attached to the shell. Available studies estimate the typical life span of a blue crab as three years or less, though a maximum age of five to eight years is possible.

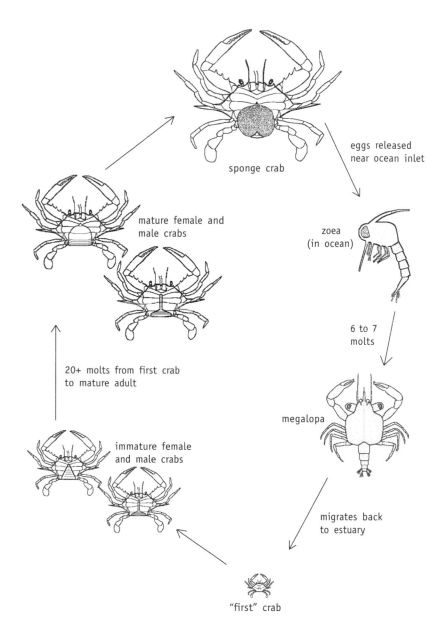

sponge crab

eggs released
near ocean inlet

mature female and
male crabs

zoea
(in ocean)

20+ molts from first crab
to mature adult

6 to 7
molts

megalopa

immature female
and male crabs

migrates back
to estuary

"first" crab

*The life cycle of a blue crab (illustrations not drawn to scale).*

## Molting

Molting is the process that enables a crab to grow. With each molt, the crab sheds it hard, outer shell (exoskeleton). The dead, non-growing shell is replaced with a new, larger-sized covering. The bigger shell allows the soft, inner body of the crab to expand and grow. With each molt, a crab increases its size by one-third or more.

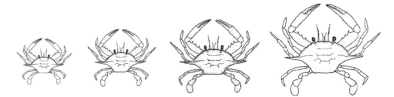

*The bigger, newly-shed crab compared with its old, molted shell.*

*Successive molts of a blue crab. With each molt, the crab increases in size by one-third or more.*

Prior to molting, the crab will consume a great deal of food, storing energy for the process. The crab locates a hiding place in shallow water, often among vegetation or debris on the bottom.

As the time for molting nears, a new shell begins to form under the crab's old shell. Subtle color changes in the second-to-last segment of the crab's swim paddles indicate how soon molting will occur: A white line indicates a molt in one to two weeks, a pink line indicates molting in three to six days, and a red line means molting in one to three days.

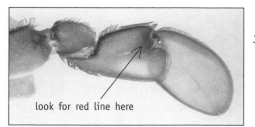

look for red line here

*Subtle color changes in the next-to-last segment of the crab's swim paddle indicate time until molting.*

The crab is known as a *peeler* right before its shell is shed.

Because even the stomach lining of the crab is lost during a molt, the crab stops feeding when molting time is very close. Some of the carbohydrates, protein, and calcium in the old shell are dissolved and stored for use in the new shell.

When the crab begins to shed, a cleavage line appears at the back of the shell, between the two swimming legs. The old shell cracks open, and the *buster* crab begins to back out of the old shell. The full process may take as long as two to three hours for a four- to five-inch crab.

The molted crab emerges in a soft-shell form. The soft-shell crab can walk and swim, but it prefers to remain in hiding, since it is defenseless until the new shell hardens. Fish, other crabs, and humans pursue soft-shell crabs with equal vigor.

The crab enters the *papershell* stage as its shell begins to harden, about 8 to 12 hours after molting. The crab resumes its full hard-shell form over the next three days.

The smallest crabs shed every 3 to 5 days, juvenile crabs every 10 to 14 days, and adult crabs every 20 to 50 days. Male crabs continue growing and molting until they die. Females usually stop molting when they reach sexual maturity (but females undergoing molts after sexual maturity have been documented). Molting is progressively more difficult for crabs as they grow larger.

The actual frequency of molting depends on food availability and water temperature: The better quality and quantity of food, and the warmer the water temperature, the more the crab will grow, and the more frequently it will molt.

## Reproduction

A female crab can mate only after her terminal (the last time in her life) molt, in the soft-shell stage.* To assure copulation in this narrow time frame, a male crab carries a female underneath

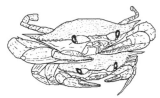

Cradling blue crabs.

him for two to three days prior to the female's molting. During this process, called cradling, the male crab holds the female with his first pair of walking legs. He defends himself, and his partner beneath him, with his claws. The pair of crabs are called a *buck and rider* or a *doubler*.

After the female sheds, mating occurs. The male and female crab join abdomen-to-abdomen. The male crab inserts two long, thin appendages, called pleopods, into corresponding pores on the female's abdomen. Mating lasts 6 to 12 hours. The male's sperm is passed in packets that are stored in seminal receptacles of the female.

A male can mate several times during his life. Mating is a once-in-a-lifetime event for a female. Mating typically occurs in the autumn.

After mating, the male continues to cradle the female, carrying her under him for several more days. The female crab is thus protected by the male until her shell hardens and she can defend herself.

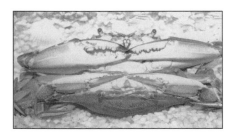

Mating blue crabs.

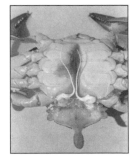

Pleopods of a male crab.

* Most sources so report. On numerous occasions, the author has observed hard-shelled females mating. Perhaps crabs, like humans, do not always follow the "rules" of their society in mating.

The female fertilizes her eggs with stored sperm the following spring. The sperm remains viable for as long as a year and it can be used for several spawnings. Thus, for blue crabs, mating and egg fertilization can occur at different times (in contrast to most marine animals in which the acts are concurrent).

When the female is ready to produce eggs, oocytes (egg cells) are sent from the ovaries into the seminal receptacles, where the eggs are fertilized by stored sperm. The female crab then places her eggs on the underside of her body, attaching them to hairy fringes on the inside of her apron. The apron wraps around the egg mass, protecting the eggs and holding them in place. The egg mass, or sponge, is bright orange at first. The sponge becomes darker as the embryos in the eggs grow and consume the egg yolk. The age of the eggs can be determined from the color of the sponge: orange-yellow = 1 to 5 days; brown = 6 to 11 days; black = 12 to 14 days. The female releases her eggs about two weeks after fertilization.

Females spawn two to five times each season. From 700,000 to 8,000,000 eggs are released each time. If a female survives predators and crab pots, she may spawn several years.

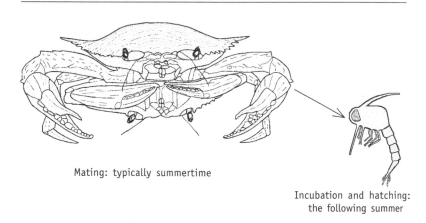

Mating: typically summertime

Incubation and hatching:
the following summer

*Most females mate during the late summer, in July, August, or September. Fertilization, incubation, and hatching are delayed until the following summer.*

## Defense Mechanisms

Blue crabs protect themselves with multiple defense mechanisms. Defenses include: 1) claws that pinch, 2) armor in the form of a hard shell with sharp spines along the edges, 3) rapid swimming, 4) swift walking, 5) camouflaging their shell through color change, 6) autotomy (limb sacrifice), and 7) burrowing into mud.

The protective benefit of the blue crab's claws is self-evident.

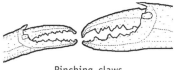

Pinching claws

Anyone who has been squeezed by the claw of an adult blue crab will testify that the pinch is powerful. A power-pinch from a blue crab's claw can inflict a painful wound, which often draws blood.

Similarly, the benefit of a hard, external shell, adorned with

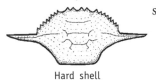

Hard shell

sharp spines and points, is obvious. Potent force must be applied to crack the crab's outer skeleton.

Combined, a blue crab's claws and spiny shell make it a formidable warrior. A blue crab has other, more subtle, tricks up its sleeve for evading predators and catching prey, as well.

A blue crab's last pair of legs, the flat, wide, oar-like paddles, are used in a circular, rowing motion to propel a blue crab

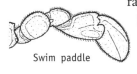

Swim paddle

rapidly through the water. Sideways swimming is the most common and fastest method of escape. A blue crab can also swim forward slowly and backward fairly rapidly, and even hover in the water.

A blue crab can move quickly on land, as well. A crab that escapes one's net or hand will scuttle quickly across a dock toward water. The crab uses both its walking legs and swim paddles to scurry sideways. The sharp spine on the side of its shell points the way as the crab moves in its sideways shuffle.

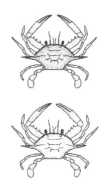

A blue crab can change the color of its shell to match the color of the background environment. A blue crab is typically dark on top in order to blend in with a dark, muddy bottom. If a blue crab is put into a light-bottomed environment, however, it will adjust the color of its exoskeleton (shell) to match the color of its surroundings. Juvenile crabs are especially adept at this camouflaging, color-changing ability.

Autotomy is the voluntary breaking off of an appendage. If a crab is attacked by a predator, the crab may sacrifice a claw, walking leg, or swim paddle. The limbs are designed to break off without injuring the crab significantly. A blood clot seals the open end of the appendage quickly (unlike a human, when an amputated leg may cause a person to bleed to death). Through a process called regeneration, a new limb grows in place of the old one. Three or more molts are required for the limb to attain near-full size.

*Autotomy and Regeneration. The crab on the far left loses its left claw to a predator, sacrificing its limb but saving its life. Over three molts, the crab is able to regrow the lost claw to a functional appendage again.*

Burrowing in mud enables a blue crab to go undetected by predators. Blue crabs burrow into the mud during their dormant period in cold weather, giving them protection. At any time during the year, though, they burrow into mud both to hunt prey and to hide themselves from animals that might prey upon them.

## Prey and Predators

Blue crabs are capable predators, capturing small worms, fish, shrimp, snails, clams, oysters, and mussels. In addition, plants such as marsh grass, eelgrass, sea lettuce, and other seaweeds are ingested. Blue crabs are sometimes cannibals: Small blue crabs are readily eaten by larger crabs. Although blue crabs are trapped by man using dead fish for bait, they are not typically scavengers, preferring live or freshly-dead food instead of stale or decaying flesh.

Blue crabs hunt by several methods. They crawl along the bottom, searching for benthic (bottom-dwelling) animals. Blue crabs also swim after and capture more mobile animals. In addition, they hunt by stealth: Using their swim paddles as shovels, they bury themselves in bottom mud or sand. There, they lie motionless until an unwary animal comes within reach. With a quick pounce, they snatch the unwary creature.

Many different animals prey on blue crabs. At least 60 species of fish are known to eat blue crabs, including red drum, seatrout, croaker, and sheepshead. Blue crabs are also eaten by gulls, herons, diving ducks, octopuses, raccoons, otters, and, of course, humans.

The hard-shell form of crabs is most often eaten by man. Hard crabs are steamed or boiled, and the meat is picked from the claws and body. Soft-shell crabs, in contrast, are eaten whole.

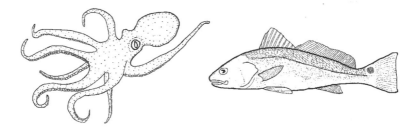

*Many animals prey on blue crabs. Crabs are one of the favorite foods of octopuses. Red drum are also known to eat their fill of blue crabs.*

## Blue Crab Hitchhikers, Parasites, and Bacteria

Numerous commensals (non-harmful hitchhikers) attach themselves to blue crabs.
Algae, barnacles (picture right), worms, slipper shells, and other animals find homes on the crab's outer shell. These external riders are shed each time a crab molts. Some barnacles also grow inside the crab's shell.

*Barnacles hitch a ride on a blue crab.*

Parasites, which can potentially harm the crab, infest crabs, too (parasites are common in humans and most animals). Small crustaceans called isopods live on the blue crab's gills or abdomen. Tiny worms and protozoans (single-celled organisms) can infect the crab's muscles.

A common, more noticeable parasite shows up as small black dots on the white meat of cooked crabs (picture below). The parasite is also visible as black dots inside the thin, translucent swim paddles of live crabs. This parasitic condition is called *pepper* or *buckshot.* Pepper occurs when flukes (microscopic, parasitic worms, *Microphallus basodactylophallus)* living in the crab are hyperparasitized by protozoans (microscopic, one-cell organisms, *Urosporidium crescens*). The fluke changes into a lesion of spores and takes on a black-dot appearance. The protozoa is spread by several species of snails that are found in low-salinity water.

*Pepper parasite on the inside of a blue crab.*

Pepper and other crab parasites are harmless to humans: The parasites are killed when the crabs are cooked.

Contrary to popular opinion, salt water is not free of germs. Bacteria are widespread in the marine environment. Some marine bacteria, especially *Vibrio* species, can cause illnesses in humans. *Vibrio* illnesses range from intestinal upset to very serious wound infections to whole-body infections that often result in death.

*Vibrio* and other bacteria reside on blue crabs (just as *Vibrio* live on many marine animals, and just as millions of bacteria live on humans).

Bacteria are not concentrated in blue crabs, as they are in filter-feeding clams and oysters. Thus, when state agencies close "shellfish" beds to harvesting, these areas are declared unsafe for harvest of oysters, clams, and mussels. Blue crabs can still be safely harvested from most of these waters.

Nevertheless, care must be taken to cook and handle crabs safely. Simple safety measures make crab consumption very safe for humans.

First, dead crabs (except fresh-frozen) should never be eaten. Dead crabs could harbor excessive bacteria or bacterial toxins.

Second, crabs must be thoroughly cooked by steaming for 20 minutes or boiling for 10 minutes. Cooking in this manner kills *Vibrio* and other bacteria, rendering them harmless.

Third, caution must be taken in handling already-cooked crabs, lest bacteria on uncooked crabs contaminate the cooked crabs. Cooked crabs should not come into contact with un-cooked crabs, nor should cooked crabs be put in a container in which live crabs have been stored. The same unwashed utensils should not be used to handle both uncooked and cooked crabs.

*Never eat dead crabs.*

# Soft-Shell Crabs

Some people mistakenly think soft-shell crabs are a different species from blue crabs. Hard-shell and soft-shell blue crabs are, of course, the same species. Soft-shells are simply freshly-molted blue crabs.

Blue crabs are delicious in the soft-shell form. They are cleaned, then eaten whole — claws, legs, swim paddles, shell, and all. Any initial squeamishness about eating a sandwich with the legs of a crab sticking out from between the pieces of bread must be put aside: The soft blue crab lives up to its scientific name (*sapidus* = tasty or savory).

Soft crabs are also nutritious. They supply ten times more edible food than hard crabs. In addition, because the shells of soft crabs contain significant calcium, they are an excellent source of this mineral.

*Soft-shell crabs are delicious and nutritious.*

Humans are not the only species to eat soft crabs: Soft-shells are stalked and eaten by numerous fish. Fishermen use this fact to advantage: Soft-shell crabs make some of the best fish bait available.

Blue crabs remain soft-shelled for only about 8 to 12 hours after molting. In this stage, the crabs are truly soft and easy to chew when cooked. In the papershell stage, the crab's new shell has begun to harden. Some restaurants serve papershells as soft-shells, but a true soft-shell is succulent and tender, not tough and chewy.

Soft crabs are most often eaten fried. Unfortunately, frying typically adds excessive fat calories, rendering a hearty seafood meal less healthy. Tasty alternatives exist: Soft-shells can be baked, broiled, grilled, stuffed, or used in soups. The recipes on pages 97 and 98 retain the excellent taste of soft crabs without adding excessive fat.

Soft-shell crabs are marketed live or fresh-frozen. Just as with hard-shell crabs, only eat fresh soft-shell crabs that are still alive. Do not eat dead crabs unless they are fresh-frozen. Fresh-frozen soft crabs are typically sold *pan ready* — the crabs have been cleaned and are ready to cook.

## Harvesting Soft-Shell Crabs

Soft-shell crabs are most often caught while seeking hard crabs (a soft bonus, so to speak).

Seeking soft-shells specifically is worthwhile, however. Soft-shells are the main fixing of a meal fit for kings.

The key to catching soft-shell crabs is to *think like a soft-shell crab.*

When a crab is ready to shed, it seeks shelter to protect itself. Eelgrass, rocks, debris, or a baitless crab pot on the bottom can all serve the crab as a place to hide during the time it sheds and while its shell hardens.

Throwing an unbaited crab pot into the water overnight sometimes results in a soft-shell crab harvest. Mating crabs often hide in a crab pot, too. Though it may seem unkind to separate crab love-bugs, the gain of both a nice-sized male and a soft-shell female is ample compensation.

Running a seine net through bottom grass often garners a soft crab or two, as well.

As an alternative, ready-to-molt crabs can be identified and kept until they molt into tasty soft-shells. The segment just above the last segment on a crab's swim paddle tells the tale. A thin line begins to show through this segment as the crab nears the time to molt. This line is part of the new shell forming underneath the old shell. If the line is white, the crab has about one to two weeks before molting. If the line is pink, about three to six days will pass prior to shedding. If the line is red, the crab is rank, meaning that molting will take place in one to three days.

| How long until shedding? Check a crab's swim paddle. | |
| --- | --- |
| white sign | one to two weeks |
| pink sign | three to six days |
| red sign (rank) | one to three days |

A crab remains a true soft-shell for only about 8 to 12 hours. The crab's shell then hardens into a firmer papershell stage. Papershell soon transforms to hard-shell.

Soft-shell crab regulations vary from state to state. Most states allow harvest of soft-shells at $3^1/2$ inches or bigger in size, rather than the 5-inch limit for hard-shell crabs. Crabbers should contact the appropriate agency to learn the regulations in the state in which they will be crabbing (phone numbers, addresses, and websites of Gulf and East Coast state agencies are listed on pages 112 to 115).

| Soft-Shell Crab Sizes | |
| --- | --- |
| medium | 3.5 to 4 inches in width |
| hotels | 4 to 4.5 inches |
| primes | 4.5 to 5 inches |
| jumbos | 5 to 5. 5 inches |
| whales or slabs | 5.5 inches or more |

## Cleaning Soft-Shell Crabs

Soft-shell crabs, unlike hard-shell crabs, must be cleaned prior to cooking. Cleaning a soft-shell crab is easier than cleaning a hard-shell crab:

1) Begin with one soft-shell crab in hand.

2) Pull back one side of the top shell from the point and remove the gray, feathery gills. Put the top shell back in place. Repeat on the other side. Discard the gills.

3) Remove the apron on the crab's underside. Discard the apron.

4) Remove the face of the crab, cutting out a small semi-circle behind the eyes. Reach into the cavity and pull out the crab's loose innards.

Rinse the crab inside and out. Put the crab on a paper towel to dry. Blot to dry further.

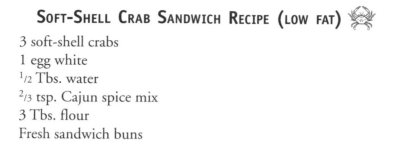

## Soft-Shell Crab Sandwich Recipe (low fat)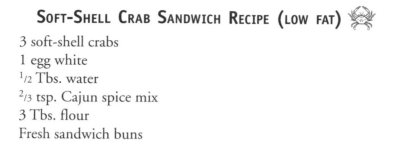

3 soft-shell crabs
1 egg white
$^1/_2$ Tbs. water
$^2/_3$ tsp. Cajun spice mix
3 Tbs. flour
Fresh sandwich buns

Mix egg white with water, using a fork. Mix flour and cajun spice in a plastic bag. Dip both sides of a crab in the egg-water mixture, then put the crab in the bag and shake the bag until the crab is covered with the flour/spice mixture. Repeat for each crab.

Spray a non-stick skillet lightly with non-stick cooking spray. Cook each side of the crabs two to three minutes over medium-high heat.

Serve each crab on a sandwich bun, slathered with cocktail sauce, and garnished with lettuce. A Cajun *GUARANTEE* (pronounced gar´-un-tee) to delight your palate if you are a soft-shell connoisseur.

The same recipe can be used to broil soft-shell crabs. When broiling, keep the crabs about six inches from the broiler, or the legs will singe black at the edges.

*Yum!*

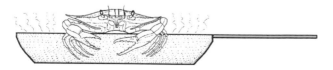

## GRILLED SOFT-SHELL CRABS

4 soft-shell crabs
2 Tbs. reduced sodium soy sauce
2 Tbs. olive oil
1 Tbs. fresh lemon juice
2 Tbs. chopped parsley

Rinse cleaned crabs with cold water. Pat dry on paper towels.

Mix ingredients. Put crabs in a large baggie or container. Pour marinade over crabs. Let crabs marinate about 30 minutes in the refrigerator.

Cook crabs for about 3 minutes per side on a hot grill. Use a smaller mesh grill to keep the crabs' legs and claws from falling down too close to the coals. Serve the crabs plain or on fresh sandwich buns.

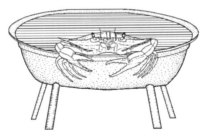

The above recipe is fairly low in fat, as little of the olive oil really remains on the crabs. An alternative, even-lower-fat marinade consists of:

4 Tbs. reduced sodium soy sauce
2 Tbs. white wine
1/2 tsp. ground ginger
1/4 tsp. ground black pepper
2 small green onions, chopped fine

Marinate 30 minutes or more, cook as above.

# Commercial Crab Harvest

The blue crab, *Callinectes sapidus*, supports a commercial seafood industry of great importance in Chesapeake Bay and along the US Southeastern and Gulf coasts. In the Chesapeake (MD, VA) and South Atlantic Coast (NC, SC, GA, FL) areas, the blue crab fishery is tops in dollar value. In the Gulf Coast (LA, TX, MS, AL), only the shrimp fishery brings in more millions of dollars.

The Chesapeake Bay comes to mind first when one mentions blue crab harvest. Actual numbers from the National Marine Fisheries Service (NMFS) confirm significant crab harvest from this area. Other states of the Atlantic and Gulf Coasts, however, now make a greater contribution to the commercial blue crab catch in the United States.

Commercial crab harvest data is available from the NMFS (see website listing, page 111) since 1950. The top five states in crab production (in order) are North Carolina, Louisiana, Maryland, Virginia, and Florida.

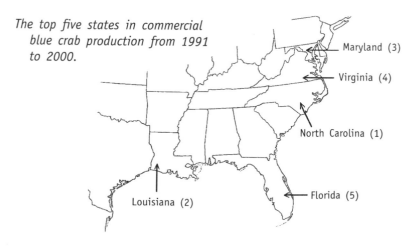

*The top five states in commercial blue crab production from 1991 to 2000.*

Maryland (3)

Virginia (4)

North Carolina (1)

Louisiana (2)

Florida (5)

The number one state in commercial crab harvest, total pounds, over the five years from 1996 to 2000 and the ten years from 1991 to 2000, was North Carolina. North Carolina, in fact, led the nation four of the five years from 1996 to 2000, averaging 57 million pounds of blue crabs harvested each year. The largest state crab harvest ever recorded was in North Carolina in 1996, with 67 million pounds caught, worth a total of $43 million.

The total US blue crab commercial catch over the five years from 1996 to 2000 averaged about 213 million pounds per year, worth about $167 million annually.

| Commercial Blue Crab Harvest (in millions of pounds) | | | | | |
|---|---|---|---|---|---|
|  | N.Carolina | Louisiana | Maryland | Virginia | Florida |
| 2000 | 40.5 | 52.0 | 22.8 | 28.8 | 11.9 |
| 1999 | 57.5 | 23.8 | 35.4 | 31.4 | 15.5 |
| 1998 | 62.1 | 43.7 | 30.9 | 34.6 | 17.2 |
| 1997 | 56.1 | 43.5 | 45.6 | 39.1 | 14.0 |
| 1996 | 67.1 | 40.0 | 40.0 | 34.2 | 16.3 |
| 1995 | 46.6 | 37.0 | 44.3 | 32.6 | 12.2 |
| 1994 | 53.5 | 36.8 | 46.6 | 35.4 | 14.2 |
| 1993 | 43.7 | 46.0 | 61.7 | 53.1 | 12.5 |
| 1992 | 41.1 | 52.0 | 30.2 | 23.9 | 14.0 |
| 1991 | 41.9 | 51.3 | 51.6 | 43.4 | 10.0 |
| 10 yr avg | 51.0 | 42.6 | 41.4 | 35.7 | 13.8 |

If the amount of blue crabs taken by amateur crabbers (estimated at $1/3$ or more of the commercial harvest) is added to the commercial harvest, about 300 million pounds of blue crabs are harvested annually in the US. Clearly, the blue crab is a resilient animal, able to maintain its population in the face of intensive fishing.

But, as with any fishery, limits exist. The blue crab fishery in the Chesapeake Bay appears to be declining. The total pounds of catch per year is slowly eroding. Studies in Maryland show that the average annual catch per crab pot dropped twenty pounds in the ten years from 1984 to 1994. In other words, commercial crabbers are using more gear and working longer hours to catch fewer crabs. The Chesapeake Bay's crabbing dominance has declined to the point that the Bay now accounts for only about one-third of the annual US commercial crab catch.

The decline in Chesapeake Bay crabbing is multifactorial; two important factors are pollution and overfishing. Much of the pollution is caused by runoff from nearby poultry and agriculture farms. The runoff contains nutrients such as nitrogen, phosphorus-rich bird droppings, and fertilizer. Excessive nutrients lead to overgrowth of algae. Algal blooms block sunlight (needed by other plant life) and reduce oxygen in the water (required by animal life).

Overfishing has been hard to control. One significant barrier in regulating the Chesapeake Bay blue crab fishery is the fact that only a single, large crab population exists in the Bay. Yet two states, Virginia and Maryland, independently regulate the fishery. Passing a regulation in both states that limits crabbing has at times been like getting a pair of hyenas to take turns feeding on a zebra carcass. In the past ten years, fisheries programs encouraging cooperation between the states have been put in place.

Natural fluctuations in crab populations make it difficult to monitor the progress of fishery controls. As with many animals, the numbers of blue crabs are cyclic from year to year. A boom year for crabs may be followed by a mediocre or even slack year(s). Time is necessary to determine if increases or decreases in crab harvests are the result of overfishing or natural factors. The question is, do we (and the crabs) have the luxury of time?

North Carolina, too, likely is overharvesting its crab population. Much of North Carolina's commercial catch is now shipped north, to the Chesapeake Bay region. This pattern is similar to the history of the oyster fishery on the East Coast: Chesapeake

Bay was first depleted of oysters. Then oyster boats moved to North Carolina and decimated the Carolina oyster beds. Oyster harvests in both Chesapeake Bay and North Carolina have yet to recover, remaining a small fraction of prior harvests. Will the same course of events follow with the blue crab fishery on the East Coast?

Optimally, commercial crab fishermen and those regulating commercial fishing should agree on a plan to maintain sustainable levels of crab harvest. If the past is any indicator, however, crab population levels and the commercial blue crab fishery will suffer miserably before action is taken.

The commercial blue crab fishery in the US is also affected by increasing competition from crab meat exported by foreign countries. The imported crab, consisting largely of pasteurized, canned crab from Asia, is sold at a cheaper price than blue crab meat produced in the US. As a result, commercial crabbers on the Atlantic and Gulf Coasts have taken a cut in the amount they are paid per bushel of crabs. Fortunately, the taste of fresh, native, blue crab is superior to the taste of imported, canned crab. This taste superiority gives American crabbers some advantage.

Fish farming has helped take the pressure off other marine species. Rockfish, flounder, shrimp, and oyster fisheries may help preserve these species in the wild.

Farming hard-shell crabs is difficult. First, crabs cannibalize their own species, so they cannot be kept in crowded conditions. Second, the blue crab life cycle involves varying salinities and temperatures (for instance, larval zoea develop best in near-ocean salinities of 26 to 33 parts salt per thousand parts water, and temperatures of 64°F to 84°F). Reproducing optimal conditions for crab development is challenging. Despite the obstacles, crab cultivation efforts are underway.

The commercial soft-shell/peeler industry has increased in size and importance over the past ten years. Soft-shell crab consumption is expected to increase as methods of harvesting and cultivating soft-shell and peeler crabs are perfected.

## Commercial Crabbing Methods

The vast majority (>95%) of crabs caught in North Carolina and Louisiana are taken with crab pots. Commercial crabbers in Chesapeake Bay also rely on crab pots for a large portion of their harvest. In addition to crab pots, Bay crabbers use trotlines and crab dredges to harvest hard crabs. Crab scrapes, peeler pounds, and holding tanks/floats are utilized in the soft crab industry.

A crab pot (picture right, see also pages 13 to 16) is a cage-like box made from steel wire galvanized with zinc. The wire is often coated with plastic for added protection. Metal reinforcing bar (rebar) is secured to the bottom of the crab pot in order to keep the pot on the bottom. A rope is securely tied to the top of the crab pot, and a Styrofoam float is secured to the near end of the rope. Multiple pots are placed and harvested daily, in open water, using a boat.

*The crab pot remains the standard for commercial crabbers.*

A trotline (diagram below, also see page 25) consists of a long strand of rope, from a hundred feet to a mile in length. Tough, inexpensive pieces of bait, such as chunks of eel or fish heads, are tied to the rope every three to four feet. Heavy chain serves to anchor both ends of the rope and keeps the trotline on the bottom. A floating buoy marks each end of the trotline.

A trotline is set daily by boat. The line is laid on the bottom in sound waters. The line is "run" every hour or so to catch crabs.

To run the line, the crabber pulls one end of the baited line up to the boat. The boat then progresses down the line, the crabber working bait-to-bait until the end of the line is reached. Crabs clinging to the baits are captured with a dip net.

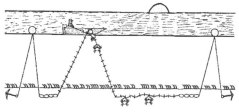

*Trotlines are still utilized by some commercial crabbers.*

A crab dredge (diagram below) is used primarily in the winter. This heavy, metal device is dragged by a boat. The mouth of the dredge is a rectangle about six feet wide. The bottom piece of the mouth has long, metal tines that rake through the muddy bottom. The tines dig up crabs from their dormant, cold-weather resting state and deposit them in a mesh bag. The dredge is very efficient, but it harvests mainly female crabs. This is because female crabs predominate in the lower Chesapeake, where dredges are commonly used.

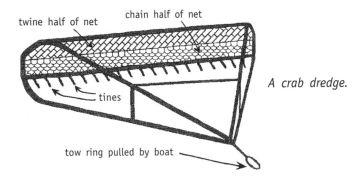

*A crab dredge.*

A crab scrape (diagram below) is used in areas where eelgrass grows on the bottom. A scrape consists of a metal rectangle about four feet wide and one foot high. A mesh net is attached to the rectangle. When the scrape is pulled behind a boat, the heavier, bottom bar scrapes along the bottom. Peeler, soft, and hard crabs, hiding in the grass, as well as the eelgrass itself, are collected in the net. The eelgrass is used as packing material for preserving and shipping the crabs. Soft crabs are then shipped live to seafood markets and restaurants.

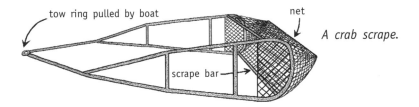

*A crab scrape.*

A peeler pound (diagrams below) consists of a lead, heart, and trap. The lead consists of a fence, made from old net webbing or mesh, that is staked in place perpendicular to a soundside shore. Crabs crawling on the bottom are directed by the lead into the funnel-like heart. The heart herds crabs into the box trap.

No bait is used in crab pounds. Pounds are designed to capture peeler crabs, but they also catch hard crabs.

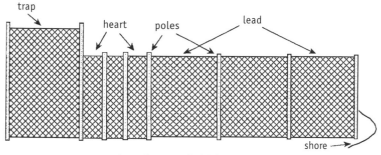

*A crab pound (side view).*

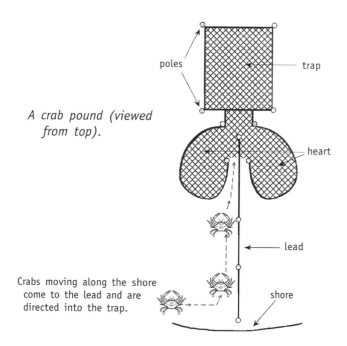

*A crab pound (viewed from top).*

Crabs moving along the shore come to the lead and are directed into the trap.

105

Soft-shell crabs, of course, are ready for market as soon as they are harvested. Increasingly, peeler crabs are sought by the crab shedding industry. Peelers are separated by signs on their swim fins as to how soon they will molt. The crabs are placed in holding floats in the water, or holding tanks on land. The crab floats/tanks are checked frequently, and newly soft-shelled crabs are removed. The soft crabs' shells cease hardening as soon as the crabs are cooled. The soft-shells are then graded according to size. They are packed and shipped, either live or frozen, to markets all over the country.

*A soft crab shedding tank. Sound water is pumped into the tank through the white, plastic pipe. Water drains back into the sound from the bottom of the tank.*

# Blue Crab Extras

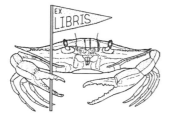

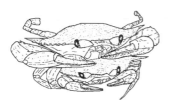

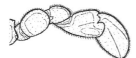

# Curious Crab Notes & Questions

1) Crab pots were developed in the Chesapeake Bay in the 1920's and 1930's. In 1938, B. F. Lewis of Harryhogan, Virginia, patented a successful design. Years passed before the design was widely accepted in other states. The same basic blueprint is still used in present-day crab pots.

2) Pennsylvania, with no saltwater touching its borders, has blue crab fishing regulations. Why? Because blue crabs enter fresh water, too. In Pennsylvania, the Delaware River harbors blue crabs. Crabs migrate upstream from briny Delaware Bay as far north as Philadelphia.

3) A female crab is reported to mate just once in her life, after her final molt. What she lacks in number she makes up in quality: Her single mating lasts 6 to 12 hours. The single mating eventually results in the fertilization of *millions* of eggs.

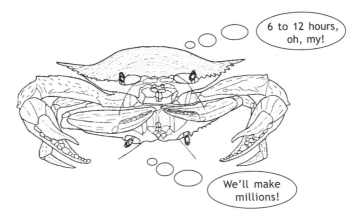

4) Female crabs usually mate in autumn. They do not fertilize and release their eggs until the next spring and summer.

5) Through research on how blue crabs and other animals regenerate appendages (sea stars – arms, lizards – tails, octopuses – arms), doctors one day might be able to help injured humans grow a new limb or a new spinal cord.

6) Chinese people labeled European lettering "crab writing" because it is done horizontally (crabs move sideways) instead of vertically like Chinese writing.

7) Crabs are delicious to eat in the soft-shell form. Lobster are not so tasty when their shell is soft because the meat is mushy.

8) The usual life of a blue crab is about three years (maximum five to eight years), while an American lobster can live 50 years or more.

9) Professional crabbers report that dead crabs in a crab pot repel live crabs. The crabbers' catch is reduced if they do not remove dead crabs from their pots. Yet, crabs have a reputation as scavengers and cannibals. Perhaps crabs have more sense than we think?

10) Blue crabs are adaptable. They survive in salinities varying from fresh water to the open ocean (36 parts salt per thousand parts water) to hypersaline (90 parts salt per thousand parts water). One thing which blue crabs do not adapt to is man's pollution; they disappear from waters that are contaminated with industrial wastes or pesticides.

11) Are you a crabby person? Do you act crab-grumpy, so sour-faced that you look like you just ate a crab apple? Are you always complaining about the crabgrass in your yard? Do you act like you suffer from crab lice infestation? If so, take a step to improve your disposition. Go crabbing!

# Recommended Reading

Capossela, Jim. *How to Catch Crabs by the Bushel.* Harrisburg, Pennsylvania: Stackpole Books, 1990.

Cottrell, Ernest. *Successful Crabbing.* Camden, Maine: International Marine Publishing Company, 1976.

Faler, Rich. *Catching & Feasting on Blue Crabs.* Greenville, Pennsylvania: Beaver Pond Publishing, 1995.

Gibbons, Euell. *Stalking the Blue-Eyed Scallop.* Chambersburg, Pennsylvania: Alan C. Hood & Co., 1964.

Guillory, Vincent. "Effect of a Terrapin Excluder Device on Blue Crab, *Callinectes sapidus,* Trap Catches," *Marine Fisheries Review.* Vol. 60, Issue 1, 1998.

Liberman, Pat and Cy. *The Crab Cookbook: How to Catch and Cook Crabs.* Moorestown, NJ: Middle Atlantic Press, 1998.

Poppke, William Randolph. *How to Catch a Crab.* Briarcliff Manor, NY: Stein and Day, 1977.

Reaske, Christopher. *The Compleat Crab and Lobster Book.* New York: Lyons & Buford, 1989.

Roberts, Russell. *All About Blue Crabs and How to Catch Them.* Grand Junction, Colorado: Centennial Publishers, 1993.

Van Engel, Willard. "The Blue Crab and its Fishery in Chesapeake Bay," *Commercial Fisheries Review,* Vol. 24, No. 9, September, 1962.

Walther, Lynette. *The Art of Catching & Cooking Crabs.* Georgetown, Delaware: William H. McCauley Publications & Imports, 1983.

Warner, William. *Beautiful Swimmers: Watermen, Crabs, and the Chesapeake Bay.* New York, NY: Penguin Books, 1976.

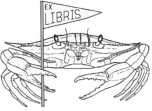

Zim, Herbert S. *Crabs.* New York: Wm. Morrow and Company, 1974.

# Recommended Websites

*Blue Crab Archives,* by Steve Zinski
http://www.blue-crab.org/

*Crabbing: All About Blue Crabs,* by Laren Leonard
http://tcomegys.tripod.com/articles/bluecrabs.htm

*NMFS Commercial Fishery Landings Data,* by National Marine
Fisheries Service
http://www.st.nmfs.noaa.gov/st1/commercial/index.html

*The Blue Crab Almanac,* by Tom Price
http://searay.50megs.com/bluecrab.html

*The Blue Crab Education Page,* by the Virginia Institute of
Marine Science (VIMS)
http://www.vims.edu/adv/ed/crab/index.html

*The Blue Crab Home Page,* by Vince Guillory
http://www.blue-crab.net/

Note: These are excellent websites, worth viewing. However,
since website addresses are subject to frequent change, the sites may
need to be located through an internet search engine.

# State Crabbing Agencies & Information Sources

## Alabama
http://www.outdooralabama.com/ – home page
http://www.outdooralabama.com/fishing/saltwater/regulations/ –
regulations
Alabama Marine Resources Division
PO Box 189, Dauphin Island, AL  36528     (334) 861-2882
PO Drawer 458, Gulf Shores, AL  36547     (251) 968-7576

## Connecticut
http://www.dep.state.ct.us/ – home page DEP
http://www.blue-crab.org/connecticut.htm – blue crabs in Connecticut
Department of Environmental Protection
79 Elm Street, Hartford, CT  06106-5127     (860) 434-6043

## Delaware
http://www.dnrec.state.de.us/dnrec2000/ – home page DFW
http://www.dnrec.state.de.us/fw/fishing.htm – regulations
http://www.blue-crab.org/delaware.htm – blue crabs in Delaware
Delaware Division of Fish & Wildlife
89 Kings Highway, Dover, DE  19901     (302) 739-5295

## Florida
http://www.floridaconservation.org//marine/ – home page
http://myfwc.com/marine/recreational/recbluecrab.htm – regulations
http://www.blue-crab.org/florida.htm – blue crabs in Florida
Florida Fish and Wildlife Conservation Commission
Division of Marine Fisheries
2590 Executive Ctr. Circle E., Ste. 201
Tallahassee, FL  32301     (850) 487-0554

## Georgia
http://www.gadnr.org/ – home page DNR and regulations
http://www.blue-crab.org/georgia.htm – blue crabs in Georgia
Georgia Department of Natural Resources
Coastal Resources Division
One Conservation Way, Brunswick, GA  31520-8687
(912) 264-7218

## Louisiana

http://www.wlf.state.la.us/apps/netgear/index.asp?cn=lawlf&pid=1 –
home page DWF
http://www.wlf.state.la.us/apps/netgear/index.asp?cn=lawlf&pid=102 –
regulations
http://www.blue-crab.org/louisiana.htm – blue crabs in Louisiana
Louisiana Department of Wildlife and Fisheries
PO Box 98000, Baton Rouge, LA  70898-9000
(985) 594-4139

## Maine

http://www.maine.gov/dmr/index.html – home page DMR
http://www.blue-crab.org/maine.htm – blue crabs in Maine
Maine Department of Marine Resources
21 State House Sta.
Augusta, ME  04333     (207) 624-6550

## Maryland

http://www.dnr.state.md.us/fisheries/ – home page DNR Fisheries
http://www.blue-crab.org/maryland.htm – blue crabs in Maryland
Maryland Department of Natural Resources, Fisheries Service
580 Taylor Avenue, Annapolis, MD  21401     (800) 688-3467

## Massachusetts

http://www.mass.gov/dfwele/dmf/index.html – home page
http://www.mass.gov/dfwele/dmf/recreationalfishing/rec_index.htm –
regulations
http://www.blue-crab.org/massachusetts.htm – blue crabs in MA
Massachusetts Division of Marine Fisheries
251 Causeway Street, Suite 400, Boston, MA  02114
(617) 626-1520

## Mississippi

http://www.dmr.state.ms.us/ – home page DMR
http://www.dmr.state.ms.us/Fisheries/crabbing.htm – regulations
http://www.blue-crab.org/mississippi.htm – blue crabs in Mississippi
Mississippi Department of Marine Resources
1141 Bayview Avenue, Suite 101, Biloxi, MS  39530
(228) 374-5022, ext. 5121

# New Jersey

http://www.state.nj.us/dep/fgw/index.htm – home page
http://www.state.nj.us/dep/fgw/blueclaw.htm – crabbing regulations
http://www.blue-crab.org/new_jersey.htm – blue crabs in NJ
New Jersey Division of Fish and Wildlife
PO Box 400
Trenton, NJ  08625-0400     (609) 292-2083

# New York

http://www.dec.state.ny.us/website/dfwmr/marine/index.htm – home
  page Bureau of Marine Resources
http://www.dec.state.ny.us/website/dfwmr/marine/finfish/swflaws.html
  – regulations
http://www.blue-crab.org/new_york.htm – blue crabs in New York
NYS DEC Finfish and Crustaceans
205 N. Belle Mead Road, Suite 1
East Setauket, NY  11733     (631) 444-0430

# North Carolina

http://www.ncfisheries.net/ – home page
http://www.ncfisheries.net/recgide.htm – recreational limits
http://www.ncfisheries.net/bluecrab/index.html – blue crab info
http://www.blue-crab.org/north_carolina.htm – blue crabs in NC
North Carolina Division of Marine Fisheries
PO Box 769
Morehead City, NC  28557
(252) 726-7021       (800) 682-2632 (in NC only)

# Rhode Island

http://www.state.ri.us/dem/ – home page
http://www.blue-crab.org/rhode_island.htm – blue crabs in RI
Dept. of Environmental Management, Division of Fish & Wildlife
4808 Tower Hill Rd.
Wakefield, RI  02879     (401) 789-3094

# South Carolina

http://www.dnr.state.sc.us/ – home page
http://www.blue-crab.org/south_carolina.htm – blue crabs in SC
South Carolina Department of Natural Resources
PO Box 167, Columbia, SC  29202     (803) 734-3888

## Texas

http://www.tpwd.state.tx.us/ – home page
http://www.tpwd.state.tx.us/publications/annual/fish/crabreg.phtml – crab regulations
http://www.tpwd.state.tx.us/fish/specinfo/crab/crabbro.phtml – crab information
http://www.blue-crab.org/texas.htm – blue crabs in Texas
Texas Parks & Wildlife
4200 Smith School Road, Austin, TX 78744
(800) 792-1112    (512) 389-4800

## Virginia

http://www.mrc.state.va.us/index.htm – home page
http://www.mrc.state.va.us/recfish&crabrules.htm – crabbing regulations
http://www.blue-crab.org/virginia.htm – blue crabs in Virginia
Virginia Marine Resources Commission, Fisheries Service
2600 Washington Avenue, 3rd floor
Newport News, VA 23607
(757) 247-2200

## Tricky Crabby Terminology

If you don't want to be labeled a *chicken-necker*, you better learn some crabber lingo! Professional crabbers have adopted numerous and varied terms for their quarry:

A mature male crab is known as a *jimmy*.

 An immature female is a *sally* or *she-crab*.

A mature female crab is called a *sook*.

 A mature female with eggs is called a *sponge* or *berry* crab.

A backfin is not a fin at all. Rather, it is the crab's rearmost appendage, or swim paddle.

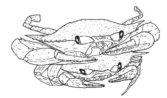 A *buck and rider* or *doubler* refers to two crabs clasped together in the cradling or mating position.

# Definitions & Crab Terms

**abdomen:** the apron of a crab, consisting of a flap folded under the body

**antenna:** long, sensory (touch, taste, smell) appendage; one antenna is located on each side of the crab's face, just inside each eyestalk

**antennule:** short, sensory (touch, taste, smell) appendage; one antennule is located on each side of the tiny, sharp, central rostrum (point) at the front of the crab's shell

**appendages:** the crab's main appendages are its ten legs (five pairs), including claws (first pair), walking legs (three pairs) and swim paddles (last pair); antennae and antennules are smaller appendages

**apron:** the abdomen of a crab, consisting of a flap folded under the body

**aquatic:** living in water

**Atlantic blue crab:** *Callinectes sapidus* is the scientific name

**autotomy:** voluntary breaking of an appendage to escape a predator (followed by regeneration of the limb)

**backfin:** the most rearward appendage, used as a swim paddle; also used to describe the select, white meat from the back of the crab's body

**bare potting:** placing an unbaited pot, designed to attract crab(s) seeking a place to hide

**berry crab:** a female crab with eggs (sponge crab)

**brackish:** water of intermediate salt content, between fresh and sea water

**buck and rider:** male and female together, during mating or when the male is cradle-carrying the female underneath him; also known as a doubler

**buckram:** a crab past the paper-shell stage but not yet in the true hard-shell stage; occurs about 24 hours after shedding

**buckshot:** crab parasite that forms black dots on the white meat; also known as pepper; cooking kills these parasites and renders the crabs safe for human consumption

**buffalo crab:** soft-shell crab with a claw(s) missing; also known as a doorknob

**buster:** a molting crab that has just begun to "bust" out of its old shell (the shell has started to split apart in back)

*Callinctes sapidus:* the scientific name of the Atlantic blue crab

**carapace:** the top part of a crab's shell, covering the crab's thorax

**channeler** or **chandler:** large male crab that remains in a deeper channel of water

**cheliped:** the first large, paired appendage of the crab, the claw

**chicken necker:** a sometimes derogatory name applied to amateur, weekend crabbers by commercial crabbers

**cradle carry:** a male carrying a female crab beneath him, in a protective "cage" he makes with his legs; occurs before and after mating

**crustacean:** class of invertebrate (no backbone) animals with a segmented body, jointed legs, and hard external shell; usually live in the water and breathe through gills

**dead man's fingers:** the gills of a crab, not edible (but not poisonous), located under the top shell

**doorknob:** soft-shell crab with a claw missing; also known as buffalo crab

**doubler:** male and female together, during mating or when the male is cradle-carrying the female underneath him; also known as a buck and rider

**estuary:** area where fresh water mixes with salt water, forming brackish water of intermediate salinity

**exoskeleton:** external skeleton or hard shell, used by an animal for protection, support, and muscle attachment

**gills:** breathing organs which extract oxygen from water; located under the crab's top shell, eight rows on each side; also known as dead man's fingers

**hard crab:** crab with a hard shell, following the buckram stage

**jimmy:** large, sexually mature, male crab

**jimmy crabbing:** male crab is tethered on a string to catch a female crab

**jimmy potting:** several jimmies are placed in the upper section of a crab pot to attract peeler female crabs that are seeking mates; no bait is used; seasonal, usually done in late May

**keeper:** a crab of legal size to harvest; in most states, the minimum legal size is 5 inches for a hard-shell crab, $3^{1}/2$ inches for a soft-shell crab

**larva:** immature form of an animal which changes shape before becoming an adult

**lateral spines:** sharp tips on either side of the crab's shell; the width of the crab is measured from the tip of one spine to the tip of the other

**lick:** a dredging run for crabs, done from a dredge boat

**megalopa:** the final larval stage of a blue crab, before it obtains the adult crab form; means "big eyes"

**molt:** process by which an animal sheds and regrows its external skeleton

**mustard:** yellow substance in a cooked crab; part of the crab's digestive system

**nicking:** breaking a small piece of a crab's claw to prevent the crab from using its claw; sometimes used to judge how close a crab is to molting

**papershell:** a crab that has passed the soft-shell stage, but before it is a buckram and hard-shell crab, about 9 to 12 hours after molting

**peeler:** a crab almost ready to shed its shell

**peeler pot:** a specially designed crab pot, with a holding cage instead of a bait box; a jimmy is placed in the holding cage, and mate-seeking, female peeler crabs enter the crab pot and are trapped; used all season long

**pepper:** crab parasite that forms black dots on the white meat; also known as buckshot; cooking kills these parasites and renders the crabs safe for human consumption

**pink sign:** a pink line inside the next-to-last segment of a crab's swim paddle, indicating a crab will molt in about 3 to 6 days

**plankton:** aquatic plants and animals that float with the tides and currents; most are microscopic; includes phytoplankton (plants) and zooplankton (animals)

**red sign:** a red line inside the next-to-last segment of a crab's swim paddle, indicating a crab will molt in about 1 to 3 days

**regeneration:** growing a new leg or claw to replace one lost to a predator

**sally:** immature female crab, with a triangular-shaped apron; also known as a she-crab

**salinity:** the saltiness of water, measured in parts per thousand; ocean water is 36/1000 (36 parts salt per thousand parts water)

**scapping:** scooping up a crab with a long-handled dip net; no bait is used

**scavenger:** an animal that feeds on dead plants and animals

**she-crab:** immature female crab; also known as a sally

**she-crab soup:** soup made with eggs from mature female crabs in sponge, not made with she-crabs (immature female crabs)

**shed:** a molt (casting off) of the external shell in order to grow

**soft crab:** crab which has just molted; the crab has a soft, pliable shell

**sook:** mature female crab, with a dome-like apron

**sponge crab:** female crab with a visible mass of eggs on her underside; the egg mass looks like a sponge; also known as a berry crab

**swimmerets:** appendages on the apron of the female crab on which the eggs are carried

**whale crab:** large soft-shell crab, 5$^{1}$/2 inches or greater

**white sign:** a white line inside the next-to-last segment of a crab's swim paddle, indicating a crab will molt in about 1 to 2 weeks

**zoea:** the initial larval stage of a crab, immediately after hatching, microscopic in size and different in form from the adult crab

## Scientific Names of Crab Species

blue crab — *Callinectes sapidus*
fiddler crab — *Uca* species
ghost crab — *Ocypode quadrata*
giant crab of Japan — *Macrocheria kaempferi*
hermit crab — *Pagurus* and *Clibanarius* species
horseshoe crab — *Limulus polyphemus*
lady crab — *Ovalipes ocellatus*
marsh crab — *Sesarma* species
mole crab — *Emerita talpoida*
oyster crab — *Pinnotheres ostreum*
spider crab — *Libinia* species
stone crab — *Menippe mercenaria*

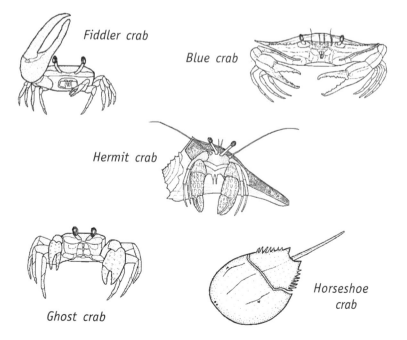

Fiddler crab

Blue crab

Hermit crab

Ghost crab

Horseshoe crab

# Index

edible crabs  73
external anatomy/appearance  76
eyes of blue crabs  77

abdomen  73
age of blue crabs  82
anatomy  76, 80
antennae  76, 78
antennules  76, 78
apron, male and female  73, 78, 79
arthropods  69
autotomy  72, 89

farming crabs  102
fiddler crab  70, 121
floaters  22
Florida  99
freezing crab meat  44

backfin  116
backfin meat  43
bacteria  92
bait for crabbing  26
barnacles  70, 91
blood  80
blue crabs  74
boiling crabs  37
box trap  17
buck and rider  86, 116
burrowing  82, 89
buster crab  85
bycatch  34

ghost crab  70, 121
ghost pots  36
giant spider crab of Japan  72, 121
gills  80

handling crabs  30
handlining  19
headlamp  21
heart of blue crab  80
hermit crab  70, 121
hibernation  82
hoop (basket) trap  18
horseshoe crab  70, 121

canned crab meat  43, 102
catching blue crabs  13
Chesapeake Bay  99-104, 108
chicken necker  26
classification of blue crab  74
claw meat  43
claws  78, 88
cleaning soft-shell crabs  96
color change  89
coloration, claws  78
commercial crab harvest  99
commercial crabbing methods  103
cooking blue crabs  37
crab pots  13, 103, 108
crab traps (hand traps)  16
cradling  86
crustaceans  69

imitation crab  43
imported crab  102
insects of the sea  71
internal anatomy  80

jimmy crab  116

kissing the bait  27
krill  70

lady crab  121
Lewis, B. F.  13, 108
life cycle  81
life span  82
lobster  70, 109
Louisiana  99
lump meat  42

dead crabs  37, 92
defense mechanisms  88
definitions & crab terms  117
deluxe meat  43
dip net  20
doubler  86, 116
dredge  104

marsh crab  70, 121
Maryland  99, 101
mating  86, 108
measuring blue crabs  32
megalopa  81
metamorphosis  71, 81
mole crab  70, 121
molting  72, 82, 84, 85

night crabbing 22
North Carolina 99, 101
nutrition - blue crab meat 46

omega-3 fatty acids 45
otter 35
oyster crab 70, 72, 121
oyster fishery 101

papershell crab 85, 93, 95
parasites 91
peeler crab 85, 106
peeler pound 105
Pennsylvania 108
pepper parasite 91
picking crabs 39
pink line 84, 95
pleopods 86
predators of blue crabs 90
prey of blue crabs 90
pyramid trap 17

range of the blue crab 74, 75
recipes 47-68, 97-98
    crab and corn chowder 56
    crab and shrimp jambalaya 64
    crab cakes 58
    crab casserole 66
    crab feast 51
    crab fingers 50
    crab New Orleans 65
    crab omelet 57
    crab pineapple delight 52
    crab salad 49
    crab salad dabs 49
    crab sandwiches 53
    crab soup 53
    crab spaghetti 60
    crab tostadas 61
    crab-cheese casserole 67
    crab-clam New England chowder 55
    crab-clam red chowder 54
    cream cheese crab dip 47
    creamy crab dip 47
    deviled crab 62
    grilled soft-shell crabs 98
    hot crab dip 48
    seafood gumbo 63
    soft-shell crab sandwich 97
    stuffed flounder 68

red line 84, 85, 95
regeneration 89, 109
regulations 31
reproduction 86, 108

salinity 29, 109
sally crab 116
scapping 21
scientific names of crab species 121
scrape 104
sea spiders 70
seafood benefits 45
season to crab 29
seine net, seining 23
setae 78
she-crab 116
shrimps 70
size measurement 32
size of blue crabs 78
size of soft-shell crabs 95
soft crab shedding tank 106
soft-shell crab recipes 97, 98
soft-shell crabs 85, 93, 94, 106
sook 116
special or flake meat 43
spider crab 121
sponge crab 87, 116
state crabbing agencies 112
steaming crabs 38
stomach 80
stone crab 70, 121
storing crabs 33
swim paddle 88, 116
swimming crabs 73

terminology of blue crabs 116, 117
terrapin, diamondback 35
trotline, trotlining 25, 103
true crabs 69, 70, 72
turtle excluder device (TED) 35

Vibrio bacteria 38, 92
Virginia 99, 101

water temperature 82
websites 111
where to crab 28
white line 84, 94
why crab 10

zoea 81

## Catch 'em, Cook 'em, Eat 'em: From whence the title came...

Much to my delight, my family has shared my curiosity and high regard for all things connected with the sea. Ben and Jason, my children, have accompanied my wife and me on shoreline excursions since they were infants. Crabbing is but one of numerous maritime activities we have pursued and enjoyed.

When Ben was eye-level to a fire hydrant, he would often traipse along with me down to our neighborhood dock to check our crab pot. Invariably, one of our neighbors would ask, "What are you going to do with those crabs, fellas?"

I could always count on Ben to answer, with only a small bit of prompting.

"Ben, what do we do with crabs?" I would query.

"Catch 'em!" came the matter-of-fact answer.

"Then what?"

"Cook 'em!" Ben would reply.

"And then what?"

"Eat 'em!" would follow.

And, catch 'em, cook 'em, and eat 'em we did!

*We caught 'em!*

# About the Author

Peter Meyer is a naturalist with an insatiable curiosity and natural affection for the environment.

Meyer has a strong academic background. He received a Bachelor of Arts degree in zoology from Miami (Ohio) University, where he was elected to Phi Beta Kappa. Meyer subsequently received a Doctor of Medicine degree from the Ohio State University, where he was elected to Alpha Omega Alpha (another academic honorary society).

Dr. Peter Meyer is board-certified in the specialty of emergency medicine. He maintains a special interest in hazardous marine animals.

Peter Meyer is also a successful writer and publisher. Other books by the author include:

• *Nature Guide to the Carolina Coast: Common Birds, Crabs, Shells, Fish, and other Entities of the Coastal Environment* (a widely-acclaimed book about the environment and common plants and animals of the Carolina coast)

• *You are the ER Doc! True-to-Life Cases for You to Treat* (an entertaining, educational, and reader-interactive presentation of emergency medicine cases for the lay public)

• *Medicalese: A Humorous Medical Dictionary* (a tongue-in-cheek, humorous look at medicine and medical terminology)

The author is pictured on page 12 and page 27 of this book.

# Nature Guide to the Carolina Coast
### Common Birds, Crabs, Shells, Fish, and other Entities of the Coastal Environment

can be ordered by mail.
Books ordered by mail are shipped promptly.

Every book ordered by mail is signed by the author.

Books can be personalized, too.
Print legibly the name of the person(s) to whom the book is to be signed
(for example, "to Bob and Sally").

Personalize to:

---

## Order form
Send a check or money order only.

Name _____

Address _____

City _____ State _____ Zip _____

Send _____ copies of *Nature Guide* at $13.95 _____

Shipping for the first book $2.00 _____

Shipping for each additional book $ .50 _____

NC residents add tax per copy of $ .98 _____

TOTAL _____

Make checks payable to: Avian-Cetacean Press
MAIL TO: **Avian-Cetacean Press**
PO Box 15643, Wilmington, NC 28408

# Blue Crabs
## Catch 'em, Cook 'em, Eat 'em
can be ordered by mail.
Books ordered by mail are shipped promptly.

Every book ordered by mail is
signed by the author.

Books can be personalized, too.
Print legibly the name of the person(s) to whom
the book is to be signed
(for example, "to Bob and Sally").

Personalize to:

---

### Order form
Send a check or money order only.

Name _____

Address_____

City_____State_____Zip_____

Send _____ copies of *Blue Crabs* at $13.95 _____

Shipping for the first book $2.00 _____

Shipping for each additional book $ .50 _____

NC residents add tax per copy of $ .98 _____

TOTAL _____

Make checks payable to: Avian-Cetacean Press
MAIL TO: **Avian-Cetacean Press**
PO Box 15643, Wilmington, NC 28408

---

# Crab-Catching Field Notes